Applying to American Universities and Colleges
for Parents and Students

Applying to American Universities and Colleges
for Parents and Students

Krystal Ann Flores

WS education

A Subsidiary of World Scientific

NEW JERSEY · LONDON · SINGAPORE · BEIJING · SHANGHAI · HONG KONG · TAIPEI · CHENNAI

Published by

WS Education Pte Ltd
5 Toh Tuck Link, Singapore 596224
USA office: 27 Warren Street, Suite 401-402, Hackensack, NJ 07601
UK office: 57 Shelton Street, Covent Garden, London WC2H 9HE

Library of Congress Cataloging-in-Publication Data
Flores, Krystal Ann, 1987–
   Applying to American Universities and Colleges for Parents and Students: Acing the App
by Krystal Ann Flores.
      pages cm
   Includes bibliographical references and index.
   ISBN 9789810758486 (softcover : alk. paper)
   1. Universities and colleges -- United States -- Admission. 2. Asian students -- United States.
3. Students, Foreign -- United States.
   LB 2351.52.U6 F575 2013
   378.1610973
                                                                            2013030511

British Library Cataloguing-in-Publication Data
A catalogue record for this book is available from the British Library.

In-house Editor: Eunice Chow

Typeset by Stallion Press
Email: enquiries@stallionpress.com

Printed in Singapore

This book is dedicated to:

Mom and Dad

Without your support, I would never be where I am
today. Thank you for always believing in me.

Mr. Scott

Thank you for guiding me throughout my four years at
Bishop Amat High School. Without a superb counselor
like you, I would not have had the college application
success I did. Thank you for continuing to be a source of
inspiration and knowledge. Thank you for being my
mentor and my friend.

And many thanks to those who made
this book possible:

Beverly Tam

Eunice Chow

Huijia Phua

Juliet Lee

Ma Chao

Contents

Preface

After living in China for a few years, I have had the opportunity to work with several different education consulting companies. I have helped market dozens of Chinese students in addition to reading hundreds of admissions essays. I have helped students based in Singapore, given advice to Korean students living in China, and counseled Asian American students in the United States. I have given tutorials on how to write resumes and how to face the American college interview process. This book is written based on close research done on the successes and failures of the different students I personally interacted with throughout different stages of the college application process.

I know that it is important to have a good college counselor in high school. Many students do not have this option. In China, college counselors are rare. In the United States, most public high schools have a ratio of far too many students for far too few counselors.

I was fortunate to find an accommodating, knowledgeable counselor at Bishop Amat Memorial High School. Without my college counselor, Mr. Scott, I knew that I would have never harnessed my full potential. He told me that if I worked hard, he would help me. Mr. Scott not only helped me to develop over four years, but also showed me that with the aid of caring advisors, students can achieve more. When I applied to college, I was accepted to 18 schools, varying from Arizona State University to Claremont McKenna College to the University of California, Berkeley to the University of Notre Dame to New York University to Yale University. I have done nearly the entire range of applications. As a college consultant, I have further studied the traits found in individuals who have made it at each level.

I am writing this book because I care. I know that the process is hard, but I want to help you and your child. This book provides useful insights, tricks and strategies on how to make the most of your situation. Please read this book to help make the college application process easier. Whether you are an international student in China or a student of Asian descent in America, this book can help you. If you are a parent, this book will make you more well-informed about the process, better enabling you to help your child or choose a company that has your best interests in mind.

1. Basics

Thousands of international students, many of whom are mainland Chinese, apply to American universities every year. If you are reading this, you or your child probably wants to apply to an American school. Although this book can be useful to most, it has specific insights directed at the mainland Chinese college applicant. Nevertheless, I will cover the following points that can help all students:

- An overview of the types of American colleges and universities.

- The basic components of most college applications.

- Insight on how to become a more competitive candidate by maximizing academic resources and activities.

- Common mistakes that mainland Chinese students (and many others) make when applying to American schools.

- Basic essentials that, when put into practice, will make you or your child a more competitive candidate.

Before we begin, there are several essentials I constantly repeat to my students. I have noticed that students who have heeded the following advice have been most successful in their college application endeavors:

Be TRUE to who YOU are

Think like an admissions reader

Write well and concisely

Write an ADMISSIONS essay not a descriptive narrative

Be HUMBLE

Useful Websites

Additionally, you will often visit the following websites before and during the college application process.

- TOEFL: http://www.ets.org/toefl/ and http://toefl.etest.net.cn/

  This is where you will find all the information you need about taking the English language placement test most suitable for American universities.

- The Common Application©: https://www.commonapp.org

  This portal allows you to apply to multiple schools from one central location. (Not all schools accept The Common App, but most do.)

- College Board: http://www.collegeboard.org/

  This website will be very useful for everything related to the SAT and Advanced Placement (AP) tests.

- Chinese Undergraduates in the United States (C U in the United States): www.cuus.org

  A great website for students by students about studying in the United States. Most of the website is comprised of forums where students can freely discuss what American universities are like and the best practices for applying to these schools.

2. For Current Applicants

Congratulations! By reading this book, you're one step closer to being accepted to the college of your dreams. Although this looks like a lot of work, do not fear! You can do it. You will do it. You will succeed and you will go to college in America. If you thoroughly read and take into consideration all the helpful hints and tricks listed here, you will be able to create a better application package.

The most useful chapters of this book to you are:

- **Basics:** Includes specifics to keep in mind before thinking about the college application process.

- **Colleges and Universities:** Provides a breakdown of the different types of colleges and universities in addition to descriptions on how difficult they are to gain acceptance into.

- **Personal Statements:** Extensive examples, do's and don'ts, and more, all focused on how to write the best essays to gain admittance to your dream college.

- **Writing the Resume and Filling Out the Activities Form:** A step-by-step guide where you learn how to describe your activities in the best light possible.

- **Letters of Recommendation:** Explains why these letters are an important part of your application and what kinds of letters will help you get in.

- **Acing the Interviews:** Do's and don'ts of interviews.

3. For Prospective Applicants and Parents

Note to Parents

Your child may be fifteen years old or your child may be three. Regardless of his or her age, this book will help you familiarize yourself with the application process so that you can best prepare your child. In addition, this chapter provides examples of how you can prepare your child for life experiences that will be most conducive when marketing him or her during the American college application process.

Note to Prospective Applicants

Congratulations on getting a head start! Whether you're eleven or fifteen, this book will be great for you and will help you prepare in the best way possible. Go to the chapters which are relevant to your age and learn how you can start preparing for both the application and success in life.

Additionally, if you are attending school in China, you can use the Test Schedule in this chapter as a guide to help make the most of your time in high school.

Note to All

Below are suggestions of activities to do at every age to prepare you or your child for success. I emphasize that these are recommendations. Each student is different and unique and will want to participate in activities that will demonstrate that uniqueness to college admissions readers. To reiterate, it is important to think about uniqueness when choosing extra-curricular activities and interests. This kind of foresight early on will make you or your child a better applicant when applying to college in the United States.

Additionally, you will note a heavy emphasis on English in my recommendations. This emphasis on obtaining as fluent as possible English speaking, writing, reading, and listening abilities is because they are necessary to get into the most prestigious schools such as Harvard University, Princeton University, Stanford University, and Yale University. Top ten schools all prefer Test Of English as a Foreign Language (TOEFL) scores over 110. Lower ranked schools will accept lower TOEFL scores. Keep this in mind as you decide how to prepare for the college application process.

Tips According to Age Groups

The following timeline is written for parents and students who hope to pursue the best colleges possible. This timeline begins at an early age because the sooner a child starts, the more prepared he or she will be. A comprehensive education in America includes a variety of activities beyond the classroom. For this reason, I have included suggestions for activities that will make students more competitive. Still, it should be noted that lower ranked schools will accept lower test scores and fewer activities. Parents and students should keep both the age of the child and school options in mind when reading this section. They should alter the following timeline according to their needs and wants. When I meet with students, I tailor or remake the following timeline according to their interests, goals and ages.

The middle school timeline is written with the mainland Chinese audience in mind.

Ages 3–4 (For Parents)

- Begin introduction to the English language. This could take the form of having your child watch English language television shows or having English language songs on. Having an English speaking tutor or an 阿姨 (*Ayi*) etc. is also a possibility if finances permit.

Acing the App

- Possibly also begin an extra-curricular activity, for example, cello, bass, and dance lessons. Uniqueness is key to the American college application process. Keep that in mind when helping direct your child to activities.

Ages 5–7 (For Parents)

- Begin English language lessons with a good English language company. It is key that your child is not only able to speak and listen, but also read and write if he or she wants to get into top schools. Find an English teaching resource that can do both.

- Make sure that your child is introduced to classic American children's books such as *The Very Hungry Caterpillar*, *Where the Wild Things Are*, *Love You Forever*, and *The Giving Tree*. Read books that will accustom him or her to American culture at an early age, which will make writing American applications easier when he or she is older (see Appendix for more examples of books to read with your child).

- Involve your child in at least one extra-curricular activity, for example, cello, bass, dance, oil painting, etc. Uniqueness and enthusiasm for an activity are central to the American college application process. Keep that in mind when helping direct your child to activities.

Ages 8–10 (For Parents)

- Make sure your child can talk about basic subjects in English. Students should also be able to write sentences and short paragraphs by this point.

- Ensure that your child is introduced to classic Western children's books appropriate to this age range, such as any books by Roald Dahl and Mercer Mayer, *Charlotte's Web*, *Number the Stars*, and others that will accustom him or her to American culture at an early age, which will make writing American applications easier when he or she is older (see Appendix for more examples of books in this age range). Remember that reading, writing and cultural understanding are all equally important if you want your child to be able to get into schools like Yale and Harvard.

- Have your child continue to be active in extra-curricular activities.

Ages 11–14 (For Parents)

- Continue with English language instruction and start to focus on writing skills.

- Make sure that your child is introduced to classic Western children's books appropriate to this age range, such as the Hardy Boys mysteries, Nancy Drew books, the Captain Underpants series, the Harry Potter series, the Percy Jackson and the Olympians series and others that will accustom him or her to American culture at an early age, which will make writing American applications easier when he or she is older (see Appendix for more examples of books for the 11 to 14 age range).

- Continue to be active in extra-curricular activities. Begin new activities that are unique and would give your child a competitive edge as an applicant.

- Send your child to summer camps or summer programs in the United States or elsewhere that either focus on English or specific skill sets.

Last Year of Junior Middle School (United States Grade 9 Equivalent)

- Begin volunteering. It is very important to see a volunteer history on resumes of college applicants. You can raise money, recycle, help at disaster relief organizations or do something else of your choosing. You should try to average at least one hour a week of volunteer work.

- Begin studying for the TOEFL.

- Read classic Western novels.

- Continue being active in extra-curricular activities, especially those that you are greatly interested in, those that are related to your choice of major, and those that will help you write a great admissions essay. You should also begin to take on leadership positions in some of these activities.

- Watch several Western television shows and movies to acclimatize yourself to the culture and learn more vocabulary.

- Get a pen pal in the United States or in other English speaking countries to practice English and learn more about Western culture.

- Take AP tests if possible.

Acing the App

- Explore the option of studying abroad at a prestigious preparatory school or other American high schools that accept foreigners instead of going to a regular high school.

First Year Senior Middle School (United States Grade 10 Equivalent)

- Ensure that you are able to compose essays in English by this point.

- Continue studying for the TOEFL. Take the test if ready.

- Begin studying for the SAT Reasoning Test and SAT Subject Tests if ready.

- Start reading books, magazines and blogs relevant to your interests.

- Stay active in extra-curricular activities and begin to take on leadership roles within these activities.

- Watch several Western television shows or movies to acclimatize yourself to the culture and learn more vocabulary.

- Continue writing to your pen pal in the United States or in other English speaking countries to practice English and learn more about Western culture.

- Begin learning a second foreign language.

- Take AP tests if possible.

- Remember that you have the option to study abroad at a prestigious preparatory school or other American high schools that accept foreigners.

Second Year Senior Middle School (United States Grade 11 Equivalent)

- Look at essay prompts for possible college choices and think about possible essay responses (during the summer).

- Continue studying for the TOEFL. Take the test if ready; retake it if necessary.

- Begin studying for the SAT Reasoning Test and SAT Subject Tests; take both if ready.

- Read books, magazines and blogs in English that are relevant to your interests.

- Learn another language.

- Take AP tests or International Baccalaureate (IB) tests if possible.

Test Schedule

Below is a brief overview of when you can take the major tests: Test Of English as a Foreign Language (TOEFL), SAT Reasoning Test (SAT I), SAT Subject Tests (SAT II), Advanced Placement (AP) tests, and International Baccalaureate (IB) tests. Refer to Chapter 5 for in-depth information on the different types of tests.

The TOEFL can be taken at any point in the process and as many times as students want to take it. Because of this, TOEFL classes can be taken at any and all times. I would encourage students to prepare and take the TOEFL as soon as possible to get it out of the way. However, students should do their best to make every test count. They should not take the test more than four times. Taking the test once or twice would be the most optimal situation.

IB tests are placed in between *'s because they can only be taken at schools with IB programs. However, AP tests can be taken alone or in conjunction with IB tests even if they are not offered at the respective schools.

Most Advanced Track

Grade	Fall
9th (初三)	Begin preparing for the SAT Reasoning Test
10th (高一)	Continue preparing for the SAT Subject Tests and AP tests; take the SAT Reasoning Test again if necessary
11th (高二)	Continue preparing for the SAT Subject Tests and AP tests *OR Begin preparing for the IB tests* Retake the SAT Subject Tests (If needed)
12th (高三)	Begin preparing for the AP tests *OR IB tests* Retake the SAT Subject Tests (If needed) *Finish college applications*
Grade	Winter
9th (初三)	Continue preparing for the SAT Reasoning Test
10th (高一)	Continue preparing for the SAT Subject Tests and AP tests; take the SAT Reasoning Test again if necessary
11th (高二)	Continue preparing for the SAT Subject Tests and AP tests *OR Begin preparing for the IB tests*
12th (高三)	Continue preparing for the AP tests *OR IB tests*

Acing the App

Grade	Spring
9th (初三)	Take the SAT Reasoning Test (It is recommended not to take it more than twice. Make sure you are prepared when you take it.)
10th (高一)	Take the SAT Subject Tests and AP tests; take the SAT Reasoning Test again if necessary
11th (高二)	Take the SAT Subject Tests and AP tests *OR IB tests*
12th (高三)	Take the AP tests *OR IB tests*

Grade	Summer
9th (初三)	Begin preparing for the SAT Subject Tests and AP tests
10th (高一)	
11th (高二)	*Begin filling out college applications*
12th (高三)	

Middle Track

Grade	Fall
9th (初三)	
10th (高一)	Begin preparing for the SAT Reasoning Test
11th (高二)	Take the SAT Reasoning Test (It is recommended not to take it more than twice. Make sure you are prepared when you take it.) Begin preparing for the SAT Subject Tests and AP tests *OR Begin preparing for the IB tests*
12th (高三)	Begin preparing for the AP tests *OR IB tests* *Finish college applications*

Grade	Winter
9th (初三)	
10th (高一)	Continue preparing for the SAT Reasoning Test
11th (高二)	Take the SAT Reasoning Test again if necessary; continue preparing for the SAT Subject Tests and AP tests *OR Begin preparing for the IB tests*
12th (高三)	Continue preparing for the AP tests *OR IB tests*

Grade	Spring
9th (初三)	
10th (高一)	Continue preparing for the SAT Reasoning Test
11th (高二)	Take the SAT Reasoning Test again if necessary OR Take the SAT Subject Tests and AP tests *OR IB tests*
12th (高三)	Take the AP tests *OR IB tests*

Grade	Summer
9th (初三)	
10th (高一)	Continue preparing for the SAT Reasoning Test
11th (高二)	Retake the SAT Subject Tests (If needed) *Begin filling out college applications*
12th (高三)	

Catch-Up Track

Grade	Fall
9th (初三)	
10th (高一)	
11th (高二)	
12th (高三)	Take the SAT Reasoning Test again if necessary Take the SAT Subject Tests Retake the SAT Subject Tests (If needed) *Finish college applications*

Grade	Winter
9th (初三)	
10th (高一)	
11th (高二)	Prepare for the SAT Reasoning Test
12th (高三)	

Grade	Spring
9th (初三)	
10th (高一)	
11th (高二)	Take the SAT Reasoning Test (It is recommended not to take it more than twice. Make sure you are prepared when you take it.)
12th (高三)	

Acing the App

Grade	Summer
9th (初三)	
10th (高一)	
11th (高二)	Continue studying for the SAT Reasoning Test Begin preparing for the SAT Subject Tests *Begin filling out college applications*
12th (高三)	

Why the Focus on Western Culture?

Since most personal statements are geared toward American applicants, it can be inferred that those who write the prompts often assume that the applicant has a satisfactory understanding of Western culture, specifically American culture. This assumption often puts foreign students at a disadvantage. Nevertheless, if combated early, students will be able to better understand tougher prompts that are based on cultural knowledge. One of the ways this is done is by exposing students to select parts of Western culture, most easily done through reading books and watching television.

For instance, I have had several students with great English speaking skills. However, their lack of knowledge pertaining to Western culture often prohibited them from performing to their full potential. My students sometimes had trouble understanding personal statement prompts or TOEFL essay questions. Other times, they did not know how to logically answer the prompts or questions. For instance, I once had a student who was asked to write about her best *Jeopardy!* category. Unfortunately, my student had never heard of *Jeopardy!* even though it is one of the most famous game shows in the United States. After explaining the concept to her, she was still not sure if she could answer the question appropriately. I watched several episodes of *Jeopardy!* with her, answering her questions throughout the process. In the end, she was able to understand the concept and write a phenomenal response.

Later, I worked with a younger student who had difficulty answering TOEFL essays. While practicing one day, he stumbled upon the following practice essay prompt from a Chinese company's TOEFL course:

> *Some people believe that it is better for people to follow ambitious dreams and goals even if they are not realistic, while others believe that people should instead focus on achieving realistic goals. Do you agree? Why or why not?*

He did not understand that he was supposed to choose to agree or disagree. He spent half of his essay writing that he did not agree, and then changed his mind later. To paraphrase, the beginning line of the last paragraph basically stated that one must accomplish realistic goals before focusing on ambitious goals. This idea is interesting and could have become a good paper. However, his poor sense of logic throughout the exercise confused the reader. From an early age, American students are taught to think about "yes" or "no" and "why". This is not as common a trend in some Asian cultures as it is in Western cultures. Thus, exposing students to specific types of Western culture can help them learn how to address these kinds of questions from an early age so that they have no problems in their later years when they take tests or apply to American universities.

Points Summarized

- Perfect your English.
- Familiarize yourself with Western culture through reading and other sources so that you can both better understand and answer personal statement prompts.
- Volunteer, intern and/or work.
- Play an instrument.
- Learn another foreign language.

4. Colleges and Universities

The different types of colleges and universities in the United States are listed below according to their general level of difficulty in gaining acceptance.

Community Colleges: These are two-year colleges that offer an Associate's degree. Community colleges are unlike most other colleges in that they do not offer four-year Bachelor's degrees. They are not as competitive to get into and have easier application forms. For someone with very low test scores and weak English speaking abilities, this could be a great college option in the United States. At community colleges, students can improve their language skills and eventually transfer to a four-year college or university. Examples of community colleges include Rio Hondo College and Cerritos College in Southern California.

State Colleges: These schools are more competitive than community colleges and offer four-year degrees. Among some of the better-known state college systems is the California State University (CSU) system. Requirements and levels of competition for admission greatly differ according to each school. Those in big cities are generally more difficult to gain entrance to than those in smaller cities. Some state colleges offer research opportunities.

State Universities: State universities vary in academic excellence. Some of these schools are among the best in the country, such as the University of California, Los Angeles or the University of Michigan at Ann Arbor. Other schools are less competitive. Generally students must have good grades, be involved in at least a few activities, and have decent scores. These schools also differ from state colleges in that they are usually more research-oriented. Most of these schools are less competitive than the Ivy Plus schools.

Private Schools: These are some of the best schools in the United States. They are similar to state universities except that they are not public institutions. Requirements for getting in are about the same as those for state universities, with several exceptions depending upon each school. Many of these are religiously affiliated, such as the University of Notre Dame in Indiana and Brandeis University in Massachusetts. Others are not religiously affiliated or are no longer affiliated to religious organizations, such as Tufts University in Massachusetts and Colgate University in New York.

The Ivy Plus Schools: These are the best of the best universities in the United States, including Harvard, Yale, Stanford, Massachusetts Institute of Technology (MIT) and many others. It is extremely competitive to get into these schools. Students must be well-rounded, active in school and in the community, have work, research or internship experiences, have extremely high SAT scores, usually have scores of 110 or above on the TOEFL, write expressive, captivating and grammatically correct personal statements, in addition to having almost perfect grades in school.

National Universities versus Liberal Arts Colleges

When most parents look at colleges, they look for specific rankings. Colleges are usually divided into two main ranking pools: national universities and liberal arts colleges. In general, national universities offer more research opportunities and more advanced degrees. Liberal arts colleges, on the other hand, are smaller schools that are more focused on the undergraduate population. Liberal arts colleges may have research opportunities and several advanced degrees, but they are generally more limited than the national universities. Both types of schools are great college options depending on what type of experience the student wishes to have.

Safety, Match and Reach Schools

Most American college counselors encourage students to apply to schools in three categories: safety, match and reach. It is advisable for students reading this book to do the same.

Safety Schools are schools that students should be able to get into easily. In order to consider a school a safety school, students must have scores and attributes well above that of the average applicant. These schools should be viewed as safe, automatic acceptances so that in case the student is denied from all other schools, he or she will have these schools to fall back on. Again, it is important to make sure the student is well above all school averages in order to consider a school a safety.

Match Schools are schools that are a match because students' test scores and attributes are equivalent to the school's profile. These are schools that students should reasonably get into, but are not necessarily guaranteed acceptances.

Reach Schools are either (a) schools that the student may not have the credentials for or (b) the elite Ivy Plus schools. These are generally schools with below 15% acceptance rates. As some say, gaining acceptance to these schools is a mix of credentials and luck. Students should apply to a few of these schools and also focus on safety and match schools unless their credentials exceed the average credentials at these schools.

Picking the Right School for You

Most international students, especially those of Chinese descent, use the *U.S. News & World Report* top 50 colleges in the United States ranking as a way of deciding on schools. However, many college counselors in the United States do not use this as a measure of whether or not a school is appropriate for a particular student. Instead, good college counselors look at the student's needs and try to pick a school that will best fulfill those needs regardless of rank.

For instance, when I had to make a decision between two colleges, my final decision was between Yale University and Arizona State University (ASU). Although I had been accepted to schools like Princeton, Dartmouth College, Notre Dame, and the University of California, Berkeley as well, my choice was not between two similarly ranked schools. I needed a school that could satisfy my intellectual curiosity, but at a reasonable price. Yale had always been my dream school, so of course it was my top choice. However, visits to ASU had shown me that I could definitely live and thrive there. ASU also accepted me into Barrett, The Honors College, a selective school for high achievers within ASU that molded students to be competitive enough so as to intellectually challenge their Ivy League peers. In the end, my financial situation worked out in a way that allowed me to pursue an education at my dream school. Nevertheless, in assessing my needs, wants, desires and hopes in a university, ASU had also been a viable option for me at that point.

Thus, in order to determine the best kind of school for yourself, you should first think about several factors:

- How good is my English if I am not a native English speaker? What schools does my TOEFL score qualify me for?

- Am I taking the SAT Reasoning Test, SAT Subject Tests or ACT? If I do not take one or more of these, will I be able to get into certain schools? If I have taken them, which schools do my scores qualify me for? Does the school I want to apply to even require that I take any of these exams?

- How are my grades at school? What is my rank in school? (Example: Am I the 13th out of 400 or the 231st out of 235? This makes a big difference.)

- Am I involved in activities at school or in the community? Do I have any leadership roles? (Involvement and leadership are needed for better schools.)

- Do I have a focus? Do I know what subject(s) I want to major in? Have I done anything in relation to this subject? Will I be able to write about why I want to do this major and how my past experiences reflect my aspirations to study this subject?

Acing the App

- What part of the United States do I want to live in? Do I want a sunny area? Do I like the snow? Do I want to be at a big school? Do I want to be at a small school? Do I want to be in a big city? Do I want to live in a small town?

Since most students either work with an agency or a college counselor, parents and students want to make sure that whoever is working with them takes the above factors into consideration. A counselor who asks these types of questions truly cares about the student and will work harder on his or her behalf.

5. Test Section

It seems that there are multiple tests to be taken when preparing for college in the United States. This chapter lists the nine most important tests in detail.

Test Of English as a Foreign Language (TOEFL)

For non-native English speaking students who want to study in the United States.

Useful links: http://www.ets.org/toefl or http://toefl.etest.net.cn/ (In Chinese)

The TOEFL measures your English listening, reading, speaking and writing abilities. The most common version of this test is scored out of 120 points. Each individual section is worth 30 points. Most Chinese students score in the 80s. Scoring in the 70s will get you into most schools. However, in order to get into the top universities, your total score should be well over 100. In addition, some less competitive colleges provide special language classes for students who were accepted with a lower score.

Students can take the TOEFL at a variety of locations multiple times a year. There is a TOEFL test almost every week. The majority of cities have it, especially provincial capitals. You must preregister for this test and pay a fee, which varies year by year. Tests fill up quickly, so be prepared to register three months or more in advance for some.

Students are encouraged to use TOEFL preparation books, work with a tutor specifically on TOEFL material, or enroll at a school or with an agency that prepares students for the TOEFL. Because there are so many different ways you can prepare for the

TOEFL on your own, I recommend that you choose one or all of the methods above as the best way to score high on the TOEFL.

International English Language Testing System (IELTS)

For non-native English speaking students who want to study in an English speaking country.

Useful link: http://www.ielts.org/

The IELTS is primarily used by British schools to assess a foreigner's English capabilities. It has two levels: Academic and General Training. Those interested in studying abroad should take the Academic level test. Since the IELTS is a British-based test, it is generally recommended that students take the TOEFL in place of the IELTS if they would like to study in the United States. However, if a student feels more comfortable with the IELTS, he or she should take it. Most American schools will still accept his or her scores on this test.

Secondary School Admissions Test (SSAT)

For international students who want to attend middle school or high school in the United States.

More and more mainland Chinese, Korean and Singaporean parents are now considering sending their children abroad for high school to facilitate their application to college in the United States. While it has not yet been proven whether this actually helps students gain acceptance, it most certainly helps that they are taking all their classes in English. In addition, American high schools also often emphasize extra-curricular activities. With better English skills, leadership positions in extra-curricular activities and good grades, international students can be more competitive college candidates if they attend school in the United States.

The SSAT is the basic middle school and high school entrance examination for non-native speakers for most schools in the United States. Note that several competitive private schools require the ISEE instead.

The SSAT has two levels:

1. Lower Level (Grades 5–7)

2. Higher Level (Grades 8–11)

Acing the App

This test has four sections:

1. Verbal: Made up of solely synonym and analogy questions to test vocabulary.

2. Math: Tests several basic Math skills, such as interpreting the information in a graph, order of operations, geometry, percentages, short word problems, and basic algebra.

3. Reading Comprehension: Almost an identical replica of the SAT reading comprehension portion, but with shorter, less difficult passages.

4. Writing Sample: Almost an identical replica of the SAT writing portion, but adjusted for age.

Since there are not many books written on nor agencies that cater to this test, it is recommended that the student finds a tutor and continues private English lessons as well.

Independent School Entrance Exam (ISEE)

For international students who would like to attend a private boarding school.

Useful link: http://erblearn.org/parents/admission/isee

The ISEE is similar to the SSAT, but it is the preferred option of The Association of Boarding Schools (TABS) in America. If a student would like to become part of the elite boarding school system, ISEE would be a better test option than the SSAT.

SAT Reasoning Test (Formerly Known as SAT I)

For students who want to attend competitive undergraduate colleges in the United States.

Useful link: http://www.collegeboard.org/

The SAT Reasoning Test is key to gaining acceptance into the top 50 colleges in the United States (though it is not required by all of them). Since many international students score reasonably high on the test, it can be said that most American colleges expect international students, especially from China, to score within a certain range. As of this year, the SAT Reasoning Test still includes Math, Critical Reading and Writing sections. 2400 is a perfect score on the SAT Reasoning Test. Each section is worth 800 points, and the test lasts for 3 hours and 45 minutes. Nevertheless, it should be noted that College Board released a statement in 2013 saying they will be significantly altering the test, especially the essay section, over the next few years. Accordingly, students who will not be taking the SAT in the next few years should refer to the College Board website to confirm whether they are taking the older, currently administered test or a new test.

Asian international students usually have almost perfect scores on the Math sections, but struggle more with the reading and writing sections. Strong scores in both sections will thus set a student apart from the others. Always remember: since international students usually score high, the higher the score the better.

Students are encouraged to use SAT Reasoning Test preparation books from an early age, work with a tutor specifically on SAT Reasoning Test material, and/or enroll at a school or agency that prepares students for the SAT Reasoning Test. The more preparation a student does, the better he or she will do on the actual test. Because there are so many different ways you can prepare for the SAT Reasoning Test on your own, I recommend that you choose one or all of the methods above as the best way to get a good score on the SAT Reasoning Test.

The majority of Asian international students take the SAT several times. It is recommended that students try the SAT Reasoning Test at least once during or before the equivalent of Grade 11 in America. Although it is offered many times throughout the year, international students typically take the SAT Reasoning Test in the months of May, June, October or December of the year they will be applying to college. The December test is often a student's last attempt to increase his or her SAT Reasoning Test score before he or she submits his or her college applications. Students may not take the SAT Reasoning Test and SAT Subject Tests on the same day. For suggestions of when it is best to take the SAT, please check the Test Schedule in Chapter 3.

The ACT

For students who want to attend most of the top 30 schools and some others.

Useful link: http://www.act.org/

Acing the App

The ACT is a common American test taking option when applying to college. The ACT is comprised of English, Mathematics, Reading and Science sections. It also offers an optional Writing section. While popular in the United States, the ACT is less popular in China, Korea, Singapore and other countries with many undergraduate applicants to American colleges. Testing agencies in China seem to have cracked the SAT Reasoning Test code and teach it much better than the ACT. For this reason, it is often encouraged that students with access to these Chinese companies take the SAT Reasoning Test over the ACT.

SAT Subject Tests (Formerly Known as SAT II)

For students who want to attend most of the top 30 schools and some others.

Useful link: http://www.collegeboard.org/

The SAT Subject Tests are not necessary for many American colleges. However, if you want to attend a top university, you will need to take at least two SAT Subject Tests. Asian international students generally obtain a perfect score of 800 when they take the Math Subject Test. Students should take subjects that reflect their academic interests. Additionally, it should be noted that the SAT Reasoning Test and SAT Subject Tests cannot be taken on the same day.

The majority of international students take the SAT Reasoning Test several times, but take the SAT Subject Tests only once. Similar to the SAT Reasoning Test, Asian international students typically take these tests in the months of May, June, October or December of the year they will be applying to college. The December test is often a student's last attempt to increase his or her SAT Subject Tests scores before he or she submits his or her college applications.

Students frequently ask whether or not they should study by themselves for these tests. While finding specific tutoring agencies for the SAT Reasoning Test is usually helpful, it is unnecessary for most SAT Subject Tests. For instance, students generally score well without guidance on the Math, Physics, Chemistry and Biology tests. However, students generally need help with non-science subjects such as English Literature,

United States History, and World History. Studying with a tutor could be recommended in these instances.

Subject test areas (in alphabetical order):

- Biology Ecological (E)

- Biology Molecular (M) (Recommended for pre-medical and Science majors)

- Chemistry

- Literature

- Languages (Various; with or without listening)

- Math Level 2 (Recommended for most colleges)

- Math Level 1

- Physics

- United States History

- World History

Advanced Placement (AP) Tests

For students who want to attend the most competitive American universities (can be taken in addition to or instead of the IB).

Useful link: http://www.collegeboard.org/

AP tests are taken during the first two weeks of May each year. These tests show colleges how prepared a student is to take college level coursework. If students score well enough, it can also get them into higher level classes once they are admitted to a university or completely exempt them from taking other classes. Students do not have to take AP courses to apply to American colleges. However, passing and high scores will help students earn admission to more selective schools. Students can also earn AP Scholar Awards. AP Scholar Awards make all students more competitive college applicants.

Acing the App

AP tests are scored on a scale of 1 to 5:

- 1: No recommendation (Not helpful)

- 2: Possibly qualified (Not helpful)

- 3: Qualified (Somewhat helpful)

- 4: Well qualified (Helpful)

- 5: Extremely well qualified (Very helpful)

AP Scholar Awards are offered if a student does particularly well. Students cannot usually be given multiple Scholar Awards. Instead, students will receive the highest award for which they qualify.

AP Scholar Awards:

- AP Scholar: At least three tests with a score of 3 or higher.

- AP Scholar with Honor: Average minimum score of 3.25 on all tests; must have a 3 or higher on at least four of these tests.

- AP Scholar with Distinction: Average minimum score of 3.5 on all tests; must have a 3 or higher on at least five of these tests.

- International AP Scholar: Awarded to the student with the best average AP score; the award is given to one male and one female student attending school outside of Canada and the United States.

- Advanced Placement International Diploma (APID): Similar to an IB Diploma, but not as difficult.

While many international high schools do not offer AP courses, it is not a problem. High school students may take AP tests any year they want without taking an AP class. It is recommended that students take an AP test after they have taken an equivalent subject at their high school. Students are encouraged to use AP preparation books, work with a tutor specifically on AP material, or enroll at a school or agency that prepares students for their AP tests. If you have trouble figuring out how or where to take AP tests, please go to the AP Tests section of the College Board website to learn more.

Since there are over 30 tests offered, it may be hard to choose which tests to take. Asian international students generally do best in Mathematics and Science-related tests. However, if a student has an interest in applying for a Humanities major, he or she should definitely take several of the Humanities-based tests. Taking a Humanities-based test like Art History or Psychology can also be used to show colleges that students are strong in a breadth of subjects.

AP tests offered (in alphabetical order):

- Art History

- Biology

- Calculus AB

- Calculus BC

- Chemistry

- Chinese Language and Culture

- Computer Science A

- English Language and Composition

- English Literature and Composition

- Environmental Science

- European History

- French Language and Culture

- German Language and Culture

- Government and Politics: Comparative

- Government and Politics: United States

- Human Geography

Acing the App

- Italian Language and Culture

- Japanese Language and Culture

- Latin

- Macroeconomics

- Microeconomics

- Music Theory

- Physics B

- Physics C: Mechanics

- Physics C: Electricity and Magnetics

- Psychology

- Spanish Language

- Spanish Literature and Culture

- Statlstics

- Studio Art: 2-D Design

- Studio Art: 3-D Design

- Studio Art: Drawing

- United States History

- World History

International Baccalaureate (IB)

For students who want to attend the most competitive American universities (interchangeable with AP testing but can also be taken in addition to AP tests).

Useful link: http://www.ibo.org/

The IB is a Western European examination system that is recognized by American universities. While it is offered as a Primary Years Programme, Middle Years Programme and Diploma Programme (senior middle school/high school), the Diploma Programme is the most relevant to a student who wants to study in America as a college student.

If students score well enough, it can get them into higher level classes once they are admitted to a university or completely exempt them from taking other classes. Students do not have to take IB tests in order to apply to American colleges; however, passing scores and high scores will help students earn admission to more selective schools. Students have the option of taking tests for an IB Diploma (more competitive) or IB Certificates (for individual subjects). IB tests are divided into Standard Level (SL) and Higher Level (HL). Unlike AP tests, students must be enrolled in an IB certified school in order to participate in the program. The IB Diploma mandates that students write an extended essay, take a Theory of Knowledge class, and do extensive volunteer work in order to complete the program. The IB Diploma Programme defines itself as a program that prepares students to be critical thinkers.

Most Asian public high schools do not offer the IB Diploma Programme. Consequently, students who participate in the program and achieve high scores may be looked upon as more favorable college admissions candidates. By going online to www.ibo.org, you can search for the nearest IB program wherever you are in the world.

Terminology and Information

IB tests can be taken in English, French and Spanish. There are also several pilot programs for taking tests in Chinese and German. Studies in language can be completed in whichever secondary language the student chooses.

Higher Level Course: A course with more teaching hours (generally 240 teaching hours or a two-year class at some schools).

Standard Level Course: A course with fewer teaching hours (generally 150 teaching hours or a one-year class at some schools).

Subject Groups: An IB Diploma student has to study six subjects. At least three of these must be studied at the Higher Level; the remaining three can be studied at the Higher Level or Lower Level. The six subject groups are:

Acing the App

- The Arts

- Mathematics and Computer Science

- Individuals and Societies

- Studies in Language and Literature

- Language Acquisition

- Experimental Sciences

Extended Essay: Required for the IB Diploma; written after the student does additional research on one of the six subjects he or she is taking.

Theory of Knowledge Class (TOK): Required for the IB Diploma; an interdisciplinary course focused on knowledge, theories of it, and ways to come to know it.

Creativity, Action, and Service (CAS): Required for the IB Diploma; the goal of this is to get students substantive experiences outside of the classroom.

6. The Common App

The Common Application© (The Common App) is the most useful tool when applying to American colleges. To view it, go to https://www.commonapp.org/. For the Fall 2013 application cycle, there will have been several substantial changes. The fourth online version of The Common App will have gone live on August 1, 2013.[1] It will no longer be offered in paper form. For this cycle, students can apply to 527 member schools. Some colleges now selectively offer applications on The Common App website; accordingly, it is a very useful tool when applying to college.

The Counselor Guide to the Application

The Common App has also uploaded a helpful Counselor Guide to the Application. This is a short two-page document that summarizes all of the main information that will be asked of students on the revised Common App. It can be used to get a general overview of what kind of information students will need to have available when filling out the main application of The Common App.

The Common App and Personal Statements

The Common App gives students multiple areas to provide examples of their writing abilities, most importantly in the personal statement and college supplement areas. These are areas to market yourself to admissions readers. For international students, content is

---

[1] Up-to-date information is not available at the time of printing.

more important than using correct grammar structures, though every attempt should be made to use proper English grammar and logic at all times.

The following is reprinted with permission of The Common App:

Instructions. The essay demonstrates your ability to write clearly and concisely on a selected topic and helps you distinguish yourself in your own voice. What do you want the readers of your application to know about you apart from courses, grades, and test scores? Choose the option that best helps you answer that question and write an essay of no more than 650 words, using the prompt to inspire and structure your response. Remember: 650 words is your limit, not your goal. Use the full range if you need it, but don't feel obligated to do so. (The application won't accept a response shorter than 250 words.)

- *Some students have a background or story that is so central to their identity that they believe their application would be incomplete without it. If this sounds like you, then please share your story.*

- *Recount an incident or time when you experienced failure. How did it affect you, and what lessons did you learn?*

- *Reflect on a time when you challenged a belief or idea. What prompted you to act? Would you make the same decision again?*

- *Describe a place or environment where you are perfectly content. What do you do or experience there, and why is it meaningful to you?*

- *Discuss an accomplishment or event, formal or informal, that marked your transition from childhood to adulthood within your culture, community, or family.*

This book offers ways to approach the personal statement on The Common App and those in the supplemental sections. For instance, many of the above essays can be answered by responding to Questions 1, 2 and 3 in Chapter 9.

The Common App has also previously included a 1,000-word section to discuss involvement in an activity; however, it should be noted that this section will no longer be included as part of the main application. Nonetheless, schools will still have the option to include some form of activity essay on their supplemental sections. If a school does in fact offer this, you should use the activity section to talk about a special activity not otherwise mentioned in your essays.

The Activities Form

The Common App also has a section for you to highlight your activities outside the classroom.

Arts and Athletics Supplemental Forms

The Common App previously had supplemental forms for arts and athletics. While the athletics supplemental will no longer be used, students will be able to submit artwork slides through www.slideroom.com or the school supplemental forms depending on the school.

Additional Information Section

Many times my students ask me what they should write here. Because of these questions, I would like to clarify that this is not an area to upload an additional essay or a brochure about yourself. Rather, if you need to explain bad grades, discuss elongated school absences or tell colleges that you are the first to attend college in your family, you write it here.

If you submit something to the additional information section, it should be a few sentences long at most. For instance, this is an area where you can describe the terms 班长 (*Banzhang*) and 课代表 (*Kedaibiao*). Many American admissions counselors have no idea what a *Banzhang* or *Kedaibiao* is and would appreciate an explanation. Please see Chapter 10 for examples of how to explain these two terms.

In general, DO NOT send in extra materials, unless the college has stated online that they will accept:

- A music clip of you playing an instrument.

- Slides of your art if you draw, paint, sketch, etc.

Several American newspapers have reported on the number of brochures colleges receive from mainland Chinese students (I have not read too much about brochures from students of other countries at this point). Almost none of these brochures are read. Most are put straight into the recycle bin. Thus, it is important to note that you should work on the application the schools ask for and not waste time on brochures. Despite my advice against creating brochures, I have had several students who have sent them in. Unfortunately, none of these brochures produced acceptance letters. If a student gets into a school, it is not because of an unread brochure, but rather because of their grades, test scores, essays, activities and recommendation letters.

7. When Should One Apply to College?

Early Decision, Early Action, Regular Decision and Rolling Admissions are the four most common ways high school students apply to college as undergraduate freshmen students. Acceptance rates are generally higher for early applicants; however, it should also be noted that admitted applicants generally exceed all average scores for the schools to which they apply. Students who stlll need to take tests in October, November or December should apply during regular decision instead of during an earlier option.

Early Decision applications are usually due November 1 though some schools now have a second round for early decision applications, like Wesleyan College in Connecticut. However, it must be noted that early decision is binding, which means students must go to the school if accepted. *U.S. News & World Report* provides a great list of the percentage of students who get in during early decision versus during regular decision at schools that offer the former.

Early Action applications are also usually due November 1. Unlike early decision, early action decisions are non-binding, so students do not have to enroll if accepted. Like with early decision, most applicants receive acceptances by mid-December. This is a better option for individuals who will also need to consider financial aid and scholarship packages in April.

There are two types of early action: restrictive and non-restrictive. Restrictive early action means a student must only apply to that school for the early cycle. Non-restrictive early action allows a student to apply to multiple schools during the early cycle. Examples of well-known schools that offer non-restrictive early action are MIT, the University of Chicago, and the University of Notre Dame. *U.S. News & World Report* provides a great list of the percentage of students who get in during early action versus during regular decision at schools that offer the former.

Regular Decision is the normal way of applying to almost all colleges. Regular decision applications are generally due either December 31 or January 1. All regular decision applicants must confirm enrollment by the national deadline date of May 1 unless otherwise specified.

Rolling Admissions is also an option at many schools. This process benefits students who have their materials and test scores prepared, enabling them to apply early. Rolling admissions applications are reviewed as they arrive. Most schools send out responses within a shorter time span than schools that do not offer rolling admissions. However, it must be noted that housing and financial aid often have stiff deadlines that must be met. The Pennsylvania State University is an example of a school that uses rolling admissions with the exception of a few specific programs within the school. Arizona State University, on the other hand, will accept applications after their priority deadline; however, they stress applying before the deadline.

8. Personal Statements

The personal statement is the most difficult section of the entire application for most Asian international students, especially mainland Chinese students. Not only does the personal statement command students to write both logical and grammatically correct sentences, it also asks them to write critically on topics they have never thought of before. For these reasons, this chapter is the longest. In this chapter, you will be provided with background information, step-by-step writing tools, and tips and tricks that will help you write better personal statements for your applications.

General Tips

- *Write about something that is meaningful to you.* Admissions officers can tell when you are genuinely excited about what you write. They like this.

- *Think about UNIQUE experiences.* I have read countless essays on the piano, basketball, Model United Nations and the Rubik's cube. This means that admissions officers are also reading innumerable essays on the same topics. A way to stand out among your peers is to write about a topic that is uncommon and unique to you.

- *Write well.* If your experiences reflect those mentioned above, that does not mean that you will not get into your dream school. Different essays on playing the piano can say a lot about a student. When comparing a dull piece to a very well written, creative essay on two students' love of the piano, an admissions officer will like the latter much more. Therefore, if your activities and answers are common for a student from your specific region, the best way to set yourself apart from the rest is to write a better essay than your peers on that subject. There will be examples of this later on.

- *Show not tell.* The phrase "show not tell" is a line repeated every day by American college counselors. It has been a mantra of the college admissions process in the United States for years now. Unfortunately, very few international students, especially those in China, have had access to this information. The classic line sums up the best kind of personal statement: it is a personal statement that shows good traits of a student through many examples rather than telling (simply stating) "I am awesome." See below for examples of show versus tell.

- *Think about your ideas in English.* When you think about them in another language, they sometimes translate awkwardly. Whenever possible, try to write and think in English.

- *Do not write a descriptive narrative.* In English writing, you must be concise. You need to have a point and provide examples to support that point. Your supporting points must follow logically. I have noticed that many mainland Chinese students write flowery pieces about their lives that do not say anything relevant to the admissions officers. Personal statements are the best way for students to market themselves to admissions officers. When writing, students should always think: will what I just wrote convince the admissions officers that I should be admitted?

- *Do not summarize books, movies, etc.* Whatever you are writing about, use it as a tool to tell the reader about you. This means *do not summarize* the stories of books, movies, video games, etc. that you are talking about. Give at most a two-sentence summary (for 500-word essays) and then talk about how that experience changed you. Admissions readers do not want to read random information; they want to get to know who you are as a person.

- *Put yourself in the shoes of an admissions reader.* When writing your essay, think from the point of view of the person admitting or denying you. Ask yourself: is this an essay that will demonstrate my ability to write well in English? Will the content of my essay persuade the admissions officer that I deserve entrance to this school? If either of these answers are "no", rewriting the essay would probably be best.

- *Write to your level.* If you are using the help of an agency or a counselor, make sure that your personal statements reflect your TOEFL score and the essay you wrote for the SAT Reasoning Test. If a student scored a 79 on his or her TOEFL, yet has personal statements that reflect a score of 111, admissions officers will notice this, disregard those essays, and possibly reject the student for this reason alone. When getting feedback on essays, students should make sure that they only include suggestions up to the point where the essay will still be believably theirs.

Common Mistakes to Avoid and How to Polish Your Essays

After having reviewed hundreds upon hundreds of essays, I have identified some of the most common and most off-putting mistakes students make. You can set yourself apart from your peers by making sure to not include these mistakes.

Mistake 1: *When writing about why you want to apply to a specific school, do not focus on common standards for American universities.* For example, since mainland Chinese students are primarily familiar with Chinese educational institutions, they often think that most of what a university offers is unique even though it may not be. In the following example taken from an actual student before counseling, I have italicized instances of this followed by a commentary in [brackets].

Question: Why do you want to go to X school?

Answer: It is never a easy way to spot a desirable university, but I am clear as what kind of university I want to attend. Compared with large universities, I wish the one for me is of *great teacher-student conversation probability*, competent for my target major of marketing and *neither far from nor centered at busy metropolis*. [Most schools in the United States boast great student-teacher ratios. If you are going to include it at all, you should find the specific ratio number on the website and write that in instead. A majority of schools also state that they are situated in a prime location that is neither too far from nor in the center of a busy city.] I am an international student with less chances to visit, I browsed the web staring a heavy mission to choose. I went down the *list of university ranking* and collected information to compare. [In general, most schools in the United States do not like to be told that a student picked them because of their ranking. Instead, universities would rather hear about the specific provisions they offer, such as special classes in a certain major or approachable teachers that contributed to that high ranking.] Among numerous possible options, I locked X University. Dedicated to reading, I learned its history of chronological development; focused to compare, I found it my best fit with *balanced academic distribution*. [Many schools claim to have a balanced academic distribution. Instead of stating this, a student should specifically describe how the academics are balanced, for example, "I like how this school requires me to not only take two Math classes, but also two writing classes so that I can have exposure to classes outside of my major."] I felt lucky for not overlooking it as my actual choice when tedious searching work almost got me randomly choosing then learning.

X University turns out to satisfy all I need. I could get easy access to anywhere around northeastern America without disturbance from big cities. Still I do not need to worry about being left behind news in a second-class city for X has *University Lectures that will invite notable figures to deliver speeches every year*. [Most schools have speaker series, so it is important to name the specific speaker series for which you are excited.] Its statistics says about a *large percentile of its faculty are doctor degree holders* with a *considerably optimum teacher-student ratio*. [In the United States, most professors have to hold doctorate degrees at the four-year university and college levels. This is not uncommon and should not be noted in an essay. Additionally, the student-faculty ratio should not be mentioned twice.] Additionally, I have time and chance to learn from them then. Even my favorite business study such as marketing specialization enjoys a long, renowned history. Everything seems so perfect and X University indeed is my choice.

Mistake 2: *If you do not entirely understand a prompt, do not attempt to write it.* A misunderstood prompt can be cause for a quick rejection. Seek the guidance of a counselor who can advise you on what it means. In the past year alone, I had dozens of students who had trouble responding to prompts because they did not understand what the question was asking. For instance, when given the prompt, "Give us your top ten list", students most times wrote an itinerary of their daily lives or listed their academic awards. Instead, a prompt like this asks for a more creative response, such as, "Tell us your top ten favorite things" or "Your top ten goals" or "Your top ten television shows". A few of my students also misunderstood a prompt regarding a coffee shop discussion. The name of the coffee shop, Campus Grounds, made the students think that the discussion would merely be taking place on campus. They completely missed that it was the name of a coffee shop and it showed in their responses. Again, if you are not 100% sure what a prompt is asking, seek the guidance of a counselor or a native English speaker.

Mistake 3: *Do not include nonsense statements.* Often times, students write statements that in their native languages make perfect sense, but when translated directly to English lack substance. Since Asian international students often write statements like these, it would be best to ask someone who is a native English speaker to review your essay. Often, non-native English speakers who are English majors in college and even some of those who have studied in the United States do not catch these mistakes. Listed below are examples from Mistake 1.

Examples:

- I browsed the web staring a heavy mission to choose.

- Among numerous possible options, I locked X University.

- I felt lucky for not overlooking it as my actual choice when tedious searching work almost got me randomly choosing then learning.

The following are examples from other students:

- Life there would be invaluable wealth.

- X University could fulfill my desire to find truths beneath the prosperity.

Mistake 4: When asked to make a rational argument for a position you do not personally support, for clarity, first state your true opinion, and then argue the opposite position. Many students have trouble with argument-based questions, especially when they ask the student to state something contrary to their beliefs. Again, if a student does not understand the prompt, he or she should seek the help of a native English speaker.

Here is an outline of how you should respond to a prompt that asks you to write an argument contrary to your personal beliefs:

i. State your true opinion HERE

ii. Write an essay in favor of the opposite position HERE

Example:

i. I hate cats. (True opinion.)

ii. Cats are the best animals in the world. They are furry, lovable and attentive creatures. (Here you write the opposite of what you believe.)

Mistake 5: Do not use improper terminology. Students sometimes write improper statements because they do not know the proper terminology. Below are some of the most frequent mistakes I have noticed and how to correct them.

Do not write "I volunteered at an old people's home" or anything similar to that phrase. In the United States, the politically correct terms to use are "elderly home", "senior citizens' home", or "convalescent home" depending on what specific work you did.

Many of my students signed "Looking forward!" as a signature in their letter to their future roommate. Generally, "Looking forward" is followed by an action.

For example, you can instead write the following:

1. Looking forward to seeing you.

2. Looking forward to meeting you.

3. Looking forward to sharing a room with you.

When using numbers, numbers under 10 should be written out as words. For numbers 10 and above, use your discretion. Either use all numerical values or all words to keep it consistent.

Do not talk about why your astrological sign will make you a good student. I have seen this trend in more essays than I would like to see. This type of reasoning does not strengthen a student's case. Instead, focus on specific traits.

Show Not Tell

Since most students do not understand how to differentiate between show and tell, I have written examples of both below. Figuring out how to turn a "tell" into a "show" will help you write better essays.

Example 1

Tell: I am awesome.

Show: I have participated in [name of organization]. As part of [name of organization], I have learned the following useful skills: [skill 1], [skill 2], and [skill 3]. I also initiated something new within the organization, which was [new initiative and description of new initiative].

Example 2

Tell: I am the most amazing Math student ever born.

Show: I am really passionate about Math. I have read the books* [name of Math book 1] and [name of Math book 2]. From these books I have learned [principle 1], [principle 2], and [principle 3]. I have applied these ideas in my research of [name of topic researched].

*Note that the Math books listed here are not textbooks, but rather theoretical books.

Example 3

Tell: I am the best piano player ever.

Show: I began learning how to play the piano when I was two years old. Since then I have won* [name of prize and name of competition 1], [name of prize and name of competition 2], [name of prize and name of competition 3] and [name of prize and name of competition 4]. I am ranked [ranking number] in the nation.

*This is something that should be included on your resume or activities list. You would not write this in a personal statement.

Example 4

Tell: I am smart.

Show: At [name of high school], I am ranked [ranking number/total students in class] in the class. I have taken [number of AP classes taken] AP classes*. My Physics teacher had trouble solving [name or type of equation] equation one time in class, but I solved it using [way equation/problem was solved].

*Again, the first part of this example should be included in your resume or activities list.

Example 5

Tell: I am a good leader.

Show: As part of [name of organization], I have been a [leadership position]. I enjoy leading my team. [Example of a student-led experience: planned a party, planned a volunteer activity, began a new initiative.]

Example 6

Tell: I am a critical thinker.

Show: I love solving complex problems. I was once fascinated by [problem/theory/concept], so I decided to read more/research more/conduct an experiment. Through my readings/research/experiment, I learned [finding]. This contributes to what I originally thought because/This refutes what I originally thought because [explanation].

The Most Common Personal Statement Topics

Although each school words its personal statement prompts differently, there are several key questions that schools ask. When I applied to almost 20 colleges, it helped me to identify which colleges were asking the same questions so that I could reuse essays. For this reason, I think it is important to teach you about the most common personal statement topics. It is always my opinion that if one can make less work for oneself while still maintaining a high caliber of work, one should. This useful trick can help all students. Therefore, each question is described below with tips on how to best answer it. Since the majority of my work has been with mainland Chinese students over the past several years, I have put together these "do's" and "don'ts" based on my interaction with them. In addition, there is room for you to practice answering these questions in the following chapter.

Before reading the essay prompts below, be aware that each question is crafted in a way to help you market yourself. Each question, no matter what it is, asks you to describe something in a way that shows yourself in a positive light and explains how you can make a contribution to that university community. With this in mind, you should write your essays in a way that would make you more likely to get into the school of your choice. While students should write about their best experiences, they should be humble when writing. They should also include specific details, but not overload their essays with unnecessary information. Additionally, describing your physical environment can be good, but you should not focus on that entirely. Read the Common Mistakes You Can Avoid section to see examples of these.

Below are some of the most common essay topics you will encounter.

In short, they are:

1. Describe an activity that you have participated in.

2. Tell us about where you come from and how this has shaped who you are.

3. Talk about an experience.

4. Why do you want to apply to X school?

5. What are you most proud of? What does this say about you?

6. What obstacles have you faced and what does overcoming these obstacles say about you?

7. Why did you pick your major and/or what are your life goals?

In depth, they are:

1. Describe an activity that you have participated in.

This question asks you to:

i. Talk about one of the most important extra-curricular activities in your life.

ii. Explain why you like or do not like this activity.

iii. Explain what you learned from this activity and how it has shaped you as a person.

iv. Give an example of a particular situation that involves this activity.

v. Discuss the impact of your leadership if you had a leadership role.

This question does not ask you to:

i. List very specific details for everything that happened in one situation regarding this activity.

ii. Write on a subject that does not answer the question.

This question is often difficult for most Asian international students because most students are encouraged to focus solely on school from a young age. As I have said before, if students want to become competitive candidates, they must participate in at least several activities. This question also stumps many students because they do not know how to write about their activity. The helpful hints above should pinpoint useful ways to discuss one's activity. For example, if a student is part of the basketball team he could talk about how being a part of a team has taught him teamwork and dedication. The student should not give too many details that do not relate, such as: *"The ball spun. It bounced and bounced to me. I could not catch it, I thought, but I did. I passed it.*

Acing the App

I watched the ball spin. It went around in the circle. My teammate passed to me. I shot. I missed..." The previous sentences do not say anything about the student. Rather, it describes an event in boring details. Instead, the student should write: *"As the ball spun towards me, I held my breath. We only had five seconds to score a point. I was nervous. Even though we lost the game in the end, I believe it was still a good learning experience. Basketball in general has been one of the most life-changing experiences of my life. Without it, I would have never learned how to be dedicated, nor would I understand team work..."* Even though both examples are only partial paragraphs, they can be used to show the difference between a good beginning and a bad beginning. While the second example does include imagery of the game, it focuses more on what was important about basketball to that student. The second example is what admissions officers prefer to see.

This type of question is commonly found in the supplemental essays of several schools. Below are two examples that will better demonstrate the difference between a good and a bad essay on this topic.

Example:
For the worst stricken area in Sichuan in 2008, I ever assisted people there with my own efforts, not by donation of money asked from parents. I could note from reports and feel the anxiety of kids there. Classroom collapsed and college entrance exam approached. At that time we were both senior-highs. Thinking they would gap a year then get a chance to attend the college entrance exam, I felt it cruel for them to suffer from loss of parents and being homeless. I had to act.

Planning to raise money, I called for class discussion seeking solutions. Finally everybody went through a census that I would be responsible for designing front pages for notebook. It was taken as kind of working, but money would be donated. I used to draw fairly well. After using up several pencils at nights, dozens of sketches of various ornamental patterns appeared on the table. That night I did not sleep. Bringing what I drew, I went to a printing house that was contacted in advance. I showed the sample pattern, both agreed then we paid for a order of 3,000 notebooks. The morning after the products were finished, and it was hot and smelled pleasant. Then the tent made up and charity sell began.

Money raised from sales of printed notebooks, with ornaments I drew, was considerable, 5 CNY each and totally we earned 15 thousand. I proposed to spend on flights inviting students suffered from earthquake, both to comfort spiritually and assist academically.

Thought it being tired, I did not do like others asking money from parents then donated. I think young adults should take some load and bear it to make others happy. It was worthwhile to see them recovering from the painful memories and energizing back on track for exams.

Notes on the essay:

This is actually a good experience to talk about. However, the entire essay demonstrates that the student has a poor command of English. The logic falters in several areas and the writer also included spelling mistakes that can be easily corrected. Some parts of this essay also appear to be translated using Google Translate. Proofreading your essay is very important for the reasons stated above. Below you will find a better example of the same story.

Better example:

The Sichuan earthquake of 2008 affected all of China in many different ways. Before this event, the idea that so many children my own age could at once become parentless and poor had never crossed my mind. After watching hours of television, the scene before me struck me with full force. I had to do something. Several of my friends suggested that we ask our parents for money so that we could make donations to different schools in Sichuan. I turned to my friends and told them that I felt it was our duty to sacrifice our time on their behalf to raise money instead of taking an easy route and just asking our parents to donate.

Finally, we decided that we would create, distribute and sell notebooks. The cover of the notebook would commemorate the strength and fortitude of the children affected by the earthquake. Some students decided to contact the printer. I was put in charge of designing the cover. I sat at my home table for hours that night. Pencils, sketches, patterns, and more littered the space around me. As dawn crept over the horizon, I gazed at the page before me, satisfied at last. I ran to the printing house to make 3,000 copies before school began. Once at school, my friends and I were able to sell all the notebooks for 5 CNY apiece, raising a total of 15,000 CNY. Although I was exhausted, I felt good at the end of the day because I was able to raise money without asking my parents for help.

2. Tell us about where you come from and how this has shaped who you are.

This question asks you to:

    i.   Talk about your background or communities you are a part of, including but not limited to geographic region, nationality, gender, religion, etc.

    ii. Give examples of specific instances or events that particularly shaped you as part of these communities.

    iii. Describe your community's significance in a larger context.

    iv. Describe how you contributed to this community.

    v.   Describe how this community has shaped you.

This question does not ask you to:

    i.   Solely emphasize your Chinese/Korean/Singaporean/etc. heritage.

    ii. Talk about how nothing has shaped you.

American universities aim to accept a diverse student body. This is a key question that will help you tell them where you come from and what subgroups they can categorize you under that will help you contribute to their university community. Since there are a multitude of students applying from each country in Asia, it is often times not enough to just identify yourself as a native of that region. For example, Chinese students frequently focus on their Chinese heritage. Asian international students must keep in mind that they are not compared to American candidates, but only to other international Asian candidates since most American schools have only so many spots for every kind of demographic they hope to include. Thus, if two students write about being Chinese, how can an admissions officer tell them apart? I usually recommend that students think smaller and talk about the region of China from which they come or their hometown. Using this topic, they can still talk about what it means to be Chinese, and also specify a locality that will resonate more with an admissions committee.

The following examples demonstrate bad and good ways in which you can answer this question.

Example:

With parents pursuing business, I almost confirmed my future in this territory. From my childhood, I see piles of business books full on shelves and undoubtedly followed as they being a mentor.

Father's gains and pains to push forward his own business set up me an vague image of business outline. Drawing a vivid and typical picture of my home, I could note the phone often rings in the midnight with voices from Japanese customers as well as those business partners. Also there would be houseguests coming to visit often, with father's passionate talking about trade policies and their concerns about cargo tariff, future and stock. At this time, my mother, as an officer in governmental department of commerce, would add new topics of latest commercial issues of the nation, commenting in a macro view. And I grow up in such conditions, breathing business air. Being led to design a way of life starts from being an entourage. I learnt from sides of business, deducing, and analyzing. All of these benefited me from convenient attempts of family business. I know the moment when I have to seek an outsider's view to think; and I mature in gradient, being confident and ambitious to succeed.

Adolescents are usually conceit egoists, I was one of them too, but with step-by-step practicality to setup my lifeline with lofty aim, though temporarily out of reach to real business operations. But I endeavored to seek a trip to university of Pennsylvania; time spent there is also an inseparable part of my world. It confirmed my future but startled with "lagged behind too far". Of this age, I have not completed the school tasks, and sometimes we are marked as blind egoists with high expectation but confined dexterity to reach. Still, I believe unrealistic dream could be the precursor of rational aspiration. Plus passion, I am willing to devote and make it come true.

Of a period plan or a long-term career of life, I would appreciate the family influence that provided my life with directions, and endowed with both practical and theoretical prerequisites. I developed my own idea to go deeper into the business frontier.

Acing the App

With current marketing skills plus what I will be exposed to in the next four years, I am confident to corporate a business as my own industrial entity. Coming next will be my perseverance and optimism to earn it.

Notes on the essay:

Awkward phrases that do not translate well into English plague the essay. The author incorporates faulty logic: he or she thinks that just because his or her parents are in business, he or she must inevitably also be involved in business. If one is to use this approach, one must do it carefully. Furthermore, the author fails to explain how exactly this has shaped who he or she has become. For instance, the author talks about a "lofty aim", but fails to mention what exactly this goal is. The author also randomly mentions a trip to the University of Pennsylvania, but fails to explain why this is relevant or what he or she did there. The author also boasts of being "confident", "ambitious", and no longer egotistical, yet gives no evidence to support these claims. Like many essays that I have read, this one essay tries to say a lot about the author without actually saying much. With proper editing and advice, this essay could turn into the essay below.

Better example:

It seems like commerce has always been a part of my world. From an early age, my parents exposed me to the nuances of business. As a baby, I crawled around piles of my father's business books. At the age of eight, I remember hearing the phone ring at midnight before my father picked it up to talk to his Japanese clients yet again. I used to sit at the table during most dinners staring at the women with shiny pins on their blouses and men in crisp business suits. Late at night, my parents would hug on the couch as they talked about cargo tariffs, stocks and international policy. Since my mother worked as an officer in the Department of Commerce, she had a lot of insight to offer.

Because of my parents' backgrounds, I feel that I have a lofty aim. I want to follow in their footsteps as a finance-minded person, but I still want to create my own path in the specific field I choose. I have decided that it is in my best interest to pursue a degree abroad because we live in a global economy. Since birth I have listened to stories about famous American entrepreneurs. My parents have reiterated that the American Dream and an American atmosphere are the reasons that people like Steve Jobs, Warren Buffet and Mark Zuckerberg exist. I admire the success of these men, but also give proper credit to the education institutions and environments that allowed them to succeed. I believe that I need to pursue a degree in the United States in order to benefit from an emboldening environment.

At dinner table conversations as a teenager, my parents engaged me. They challenged me to think about business from economic, marketing and cultural perspectives. Because of this upbringing, I hope to have the opportunity to explore business in similar ways in the United States. Should I remain in China and choose to study at a Chinese university, I would be unable to find this kind of exposure. As a passionate, ambitious student, I hope to be challenged and inspired as an Economics major at the University of Pennsylvania.

3. Talk about an experience.

This question asks you to:

    i.   Discuss an activity or event in your life that is significant.

    ii.   Explain what the significance of this experience is to you.

This question does not ask you to:

    i.   Discuss a random event or activity.

    ii.   Write about a nature scene.

As you can see, there is a general theme to admissions essays. Most personal statements ask students to write about something significant that has shaped them in some way. This one uses an "experience" as a vehicle for students to describe themselves and their intellectual curiosity. Asian international students should use this kind of open-ended question to write about an experience that makes them seem like a more appealing character. For example:

- If a student wants to major in Biology he could talk about an experience in the laboratory that first awakened his love of Biology.

Acing the App

- Another student who wants to major in History or Literature can talk about reading her favorite book and how this encouraged her to consider her major.

- A student who loves playing the violin could talk about the first violin concert she went to when she was five that inspired her to begin playing.

- A student who wants to go into finance can talk about going to work with her father occasionally and learning the ins and outs of international trade or how she started her own Taobao or eBay page, learning about sales, profits, and revenue on her own.

- Another student who wants to continue participating in volunteer work in college could write about his volunteer trips to a poor southern region that have time and time again reaffirmed the importance of community engagement in his mind.

- A student who was saddened by the death of her grandmother could write about how that experience convinced her to evoke the positive personality traits of her grandmother in her daily life. In this way, her grandmother would live through her.

The examples below can show you both a good and bad example of how to answer this question.

Example:

In China, Model United Nations is not so highly regarded as in other places. But I have always enjoyed being part of multi-cultural interactions, and so when given the chance I eagerly joined my school's chapter. From the very start I enjoyed the discussions and debates about a wide variety of issues. I liked to try and view a given issue from the perspective of the different countries involved. That way the agreements and differences could be separated and the process of resolution or compromise begun.

It wasn't long however, before the first interschool conference was scheduled. The enthusiasm that had put me in a leadership position at my school came with the responsibility of having to give an important presentation in front of many people. I would have liked to pass of the responsibility, but it was mine to bear.

I dealt with the nervousness of anticipation by throwing myself fully into preparation. I first researched the issue I was meant to present, examining it from different perspectives, hoping I could present the facts clearly will also mentioning the potential contentious aspects. Once my material was prepared I began the more unfamiliar task of preparing to present it publicly.

I read other speeches, watched other performances and tried to imitate their style, hoping to keep the effectiveness. But I always found myself feeling awkward and unnatural. Out of a desperate lack of ideas, I decided I would just present my case plainly.

Standing on the edge of the stage, hundreds of people in the audience, my nervousness peaked. I had never imagined that even walking to the podium would be hard, my knees wobbled. The first words out of my mouth also were shaky. Terrified of my surrounding I just focused on speaking the words I had prepared. Before I knew it my speech had passed, I walked off stage and relief overcame me. Immediately, people I did not know gave me approving glances or even congratulated me saying I had done well. My relief turned to pride in facing my fear successfully.

In the later discussion and debate I felt much more confident, in my research as always, but also in my ability to express it. Seeing my words understood and effective I was further emboldened. My new found confidence was liberating. It helped me not only discuss issues at hand but make new friends in between the scheduled events.

I used to think of public speaking as an activity to be dodged, it was much too uncomfortable for me. After this experience, I realized it can be an exhilarating experience in itself. What's more, for a girl who wants to make a career facilitating between cultures, this method of communication is invaluable. The confidence it gives me also helps me communicate better in other ways as well. Now that I have conquered my fear I look forward to improving my style.

Notes on the essay:
This essay is generally better written than most first attempt essays I have seen. The student explains her experience and its impact on her. However, with advice, the essay above could turn into the essay below.

Acing the App

Better example:

Standing on the edge of the stage with hundreds of people in the audience, my nervousness peaked. I had never imagined that even walking to the podium would be so hard. My knees wobbled and the first words out of my mouth were shaky. Yet, I continued to speak. My Model United Nations (MUN) delegation depended on me.

MUN was a fascinating, eye-opening experience for me. In my opinion, it is one of the few times when Chinese students are given the opportunity to be vocal about world issues and conflict resolution. As someone who hopes to serve as a conduit between cultures in the future, I joined MUN in high school because I believed it would help me build the skills necessary to achieve my future dream.

Despite wanting to learn public speaking skills, I feared giving presentations in the beginning. Each of my first few conferences made me so anxious that I would spend hours preparing. Since I realized that communication is an invaluable asset when working with others and that I needed to master it, I read famous speeches, watched speakers on TED talks, noted their styles, imitated them, and hoped to achieve my desired effect. Unfortunately, I always felt awkward and unnatural after trying to imitate these phenomenal speakers. Eventually I decided to just present my case plainly because it would best suit who I am.

Over time, I developed confidence when speaking. My new found confidence was liberating. I used to think of public speaking as an activity to be dodged since it often made me feel uncomfortable. Now that I have conquered my fear I look forward to improving my style.

My interest and investment in MUN drew the attention of my peers. In the end, they elected me a leader among the group. Now, I not only derive enjoyment from MUN, but would also learn responsibility. MUN has helped me to grow and develop as a person. Without it, I would not be the confident, imaginative student that I am.

4. Why do you want to apply to X school?

This question asks you to:

    i. Discuss concrete reasons about why you want to apply to that school.

ii. Talk about a strong department you would like to do your major in.

iii. Talk about specific professors with whom you would like to take classes or with whom you would like to perform research.

iv. Discuss their approach to education and how it aligns with your beliefs on education.

v. Discuss how their approach to education will help you achieve your goals.

vi. Discuss programs, internships, clubs or organizations unique to that school.

vii. Discuss the benefits of the location or atmosphere offered by the school.

viii. Acknowledge previous visits to the school (if any).

ix. Talk about people you know who are students or alumni of the school (if written correctly).

This question does not ask you to:

i. Tell them you are applying because they have a high ranking.

ii. List abstract details that can be used to describe any school.

iii. Paste long quotes from their website.

iv. Talk about people you know who are students or alumni of the school (if written inappropriately).

This is the most common supplemental essay on The Common App because most universities want to know why you chose to apply there. All schools want an original answer. Basically, this essay shows whether or not you have done your research on the school. In order to impress admissions officers, learn as much as you can and then write about which parts specifically affect your goals and aspirations. Think of this essay as yin and yang. One part must complete the other. Try to show these schools that what they offer fits in perfectly with what you need. Good phrases to use are: "X about this school will help me achieve my goal of Z", or "Without X, I know I will never learn as much as I need to about Z", or "The X program will help me to develop A, B, and C traits".

Acing the App

The examples below can show you both a good and bad example of how to answer this question.

Example:

Curiosity in childhood drove me to ask questions, then it developed to be such a strong desire that I tried to understand every line in chemistry and biology textbooks, exercise pamphlets and materials beyond classroom.

Given chance to study in an international high school, I could get easy access to AP courses in which scientific subjects are my favorite. With a considerable English vocabulary, I could read through the web the latest fruits and news in endeavors of biology and chemistry.

Inspired by what I saw in hospital, I would dash my pen on the application form and go for biochemistry. As a hose for multiple disciplines, USC will give their cutting edge advantages as well as chances to combine them as integrity. I consider myself the one that will benefit most from this policy, absorbing from both biology and chemistry all at once. Lectures, labs even field surveys would be ideal learning routines for me. I could enhance what I learn from classroom by pursuing concrete experiments, see it and feel it. Or another academic schedule, I could dive into chemistry for a postgraduate after a full and intensive study of biology, different routes, but the same goal.

Notes on the essay:

This essay gives random glimpses into the student's mind. While better than most of the essays I've seen on "why X school" and "why Z major", it is still very scattered and does not follow logically. It also suffers from many instances where the Chinese has been directly translated into English without looking to see if the specific translation makes sense.

Better example:

Unlike most Chinese students, Yale's ranking on the *U.S. News & World Report* does not matter to me. I want to go to Yale University for three specific reasons. First and most importantly, I want to go to Yale because I feel the rigor of its academics and emphasis on connecting the Sciences and the Humanities will help me develop into a more inquisitive and knowledgeable human being. Additionally, since I want to major in Computer Science with an emphasis on Internet security, I think Yale is perfect for me. In the age of Anonymous, the Security and Cryptology department at Yale will help me directly target my interest. I am also a fan of Joan Feigenbaum and Zhong Shao's research. I would be delighted to have the opportunity to perform research with them. Additionally, Yale's Grand Strategy course led by a team of Grand Strategy masters intrigues me. I feel that my concentration within the major would contribute to a better discussion in a highly pertinent field.

Second, there is an abundance of extra-curricular activities. Since I have participated in choir all my life, I hope to attend a school renowned for its a cappella groups. Yale has over 15 a cappella groups, among them Whim 'n Rhythm, which I would aspire to be part of as a senior. Yale also boasts a fairly active and reputed tennis team. I have played tennis since the age of four and would like to continue playing on the Yale Club Tennis team. Third, few American universities boast the unifying residential college system. When searching for colleges, I made sure to look for only those that would offer this immediate sense of community. In reading about Yale online, every student seems to emphasize that they feel they have found a family atmosphere at Yale because of the residential college system. I want an organized and encouraging structure like this to support me throughout my four years of undergraduate study.

5. What are you most proud of? What does this say about you?

This question asks you to:

    i.   List a personality characteristic or accomplishment.

    ii.   Relate this quality or experience to your ability to do the same in the future.

    iii.   Discuss why this trait or accomplishment is most important to you.

This question does not ask you to:

    i.   Talk about how you are the best at something.

    ii.   Gloat or boast.

Unfortunately, I have seen many students use this as an opportunity to boast about themselves. This question actually asks students to think critically about their lives and write an insightful piece. This question is even hard for American applicants. For these reasons, I give the following advice. Students can easily write about an award they won. In this instance, students should focus on the dedication and preparation that went into winning that award and concentrate less on the feeling of success afterwards. Admissions officers prefer to see essays that emphasize the process and what a student learned along the way. Students can write about being proud of a personal trait, like being charismatic or dedicated and then share how this has affected them or why they think this is important. Students can also write about moral dilemmas. In this situation, students should be wary to not speak too negatively. They should instead focus on how the situation was an opportunity for them to help others and grow. Furthermore, students can write about volunteer activities, getting better in a class that was extremely hard, and a multitude of other things. The best way to figure out what to write about is for students to ask themselves of all the accomplishments in their life, of which are they most proud? Then they should proceed to write about their accomplishments in a humble way that will interest the admissions reader.

The examples below can show you both a good and bad example of how to answer this question.

Example:
As early as my childhood, toys were still car models and Barbie dolls. But what I felt proud of was none of them, the too childish toys without intelligence. I always fond of complicated things, because it could push me to be smarter. This was one of the qualities that distinguish me from other kids at that time. It was exciting when father bought me a Rubik's cube. But it was also my first frustrating toy. This puzzle of rotatable pieces confused me not able to patch all six faces. But I enjoyed completing one face again and again.

Reading instructions thoroughly, I just sat there alone and cared nothing but this cube full of colored stickers. Cyclopedias gave me helpful tips, from which I knew various ways of rotating the cubelets. Finally it was cracked with stickers of each color gathered in each face, and rewarded me with qualities for life use. I know some Latin language, and Meliora best describes me "to be a better man". For me I would rather make it Meliorare, the plural form, by taking action to research and refine what I know, like what I contributed with my mind to the cube.

Notes on the essay:

As I have previously mentioned, many mainland Chinese students write about the Rubik's cube. Thus, if a student is to write about it, the essay must be phenomenal. This essay attempts to show the development of the student because of the Rubik's cube, but it fails to show why it is meaningful. Then, the student makes a last ditch attempt to include "Meliora", the motto of the school, while failing to make it connect to his overall essay theme.

Better example:

Since childhood, the idea of complexity fascinated me. Like many other Chinese students, my parents put a Rubik's cube in my hand at an early age. With every rotation of a face or unlocking of the puzzle, I felt inspired. Unlike most Chinese students, however, my parents gave me a paintbrush too. I stimulated my mathematical side through playing with the Rubik's cube and my artistic side with oil painting classes. While walking along the art shops at 798, a well-known art district in Beijing, I came across Rubik's cubes used as art. This experience changed my life forever.

I bought a hundred Rubik's cubes and began to assemble them into pictures like the one I had seen in 798. I had to rotate each cube until its main face presented the right combination of colors that I needed to finish the cheeks or hands that I created. I later went on to create pictures of plants, animals and scientific equipment with my forever growing set of Rubik's cubes.

During the Chinese equivalent of 8th grade, I entered an art contest. I titled my piece "The Intersection of Precision and Art". I won first prize. That award still hangs on my bookshelf. I look at it every day and remind myself that in order to be a complete person, I must look at things from many different sides. It is my Meliora, a constant reminder that I must continue to better myself by being perceptive. To me, a Rubik's cube is not just a Rubik's cube and art not only consists of paintings. Instead, a Rubik's cube can become art.

Acing the App

6. What obstacles have you faced and what does overcoming these obstacles say about you?

This question asks you to:

    i.   Think about the real difficulties in your life.

    ii. Figure out how these obstacles have contributed to making you a better person in some way.

This question does not ask you to:

    i.   Say you have faced no obstacles.

This is a relatively straightforward, easy essay prompt. Students can talk about a class or an activity they struggled with. These essays should always end on a positive, upbeat note. See examples below of what to write and what not to write.

Example:

Basketball had been a faithful companion since I was in middle school. I thought puberty had endowed me with a physical advantage, being tall and strong enough to take it as my item of sports. Confidently rushing into a sportswear store, I bought a basketball, clean but still not puffed. The moment reminded me that actually I was it, knowing little court rules and even unable to perform a cross-leg dribble. But I was then proud of myself, enacting it by buying it. However I loved it, it also repelled me, when I went for competition with those professionals, and I knew what was sarcasm and how much improvements I needed. Even for some time I hesitated to give it up.

Being it a boy's symbol, I remember it was popular for boys to clip a basketball at the rear rack of the bike, and then pedal to school. I carried the basketball to the field and offered those unknown players a request to join. Surprised by their rebounds and three-pointers, I started to bounce the ball and dribble, but still with eyes on hands and the ball, not like them watching around with alert, striding with skillful domination. I even hit the ball on toes and it bounced away. That was my first on-field trial that made me aware of difference.

I constantly played with classmates, still not a match. Even if there were improvements in small paces, I was still the one below average performance. They would dismiss gradually upon I showed up at the field. One of them even said once "Join us when you are good!" I could note they just jokingly said it without anything serious or intent to hurt, but it was no longer the soft refusal of dismiss, but I really need to improve. What significance for a beginner to have a context to learn! But I was not given one; all I had to do was to stand out by self-efforts. Still that bike carrying basketball, I rode it to playground to sweat off my vest. Most of my spare time was scheduled for practice. Even it was winter the coldness would not freeze my fingers to feel the basketball, and make shots. NBA live shows occupied the rest of the schedule, teaching me new moves and skills. Now I have learned a lot, that a player's weight is as important as his stature, hence I came to serve as a center in varsity to offer as best as I can.

With a passion could friends be made, but not get dispelled by it. Off each match, I would be an advisor in court, teaching students like I used to have dreams. All I could do is to offer a environment, but not leave them alone frustrated.

Notes on the essay:
While this essay presents a real obstacle, the author forgets to mention the outcome of him overcoming his obstacle (becoming better in basketball). The student spends too much time describing the obstacle and not enough time explaining the importance in overcoming it. The way in which and the reasons why one tries to overcome obstacles are usually much more important than the obstacle itself to admissions officers. They hope to learn more about your personality by observing how you approach difficult situations.

Better example:
I stood at the edge of the court with a basketball in my hand. Behind me were a row of bikes, all of them equipped with a special clip to keep a basketball steady in their basket while the bike was being ridden. I turned to look at my bike among that line of bikes. Something inside of me wanted to bolt back, hop on and ride away. Something inside me also melted my feet to the ground, preventing me from moving in any direction.

Basketball is a symbol for boys in China. After I hit puberty, I felt endowed with a special physical advantage. My body, unlike that of most of my peers, reached upward towards the basketball net. I believed that with this newfound height and strength, I could now become the basketball star I had always dreamed about becoming.

Acing the App

One day I pedaled to a sports store after school. I bought a beautiful, bright orange basketball and pumped it myself. I told myself that the next day I would go to the basketball court and try to play with the guys known as "ballers" at my high school. Now that I was before them, I was frozen. I did not know what to do or say. Eventually when the ball hit me as I stood there at the edge, one of the basketball players made fun of me. This woke me up. I turned to the player next to the one who had criticized me. I asked him if I could join.

Their soft shots and hard rebounds surprised me. The finesse with which they moved about enraptured me. Try as I might, my skills could not match theirs. After playing that day, I walked home with my head bowed down in shame. I could not believe that I had believed myself capable of taking on the ballers just because I was tall.

I do not know why I returned the next day. After I shot an air ball, someone called to me, "Hey, come back again when you figure out where the hoop is." Although that remark and others like it hurt, I continued to come back. I began to watch NBA Live every day. I noticed the traits that allowed several key players to dominate. I also spent more time at the gym. I began lifting weights to become stronger. I then spent hours on the basketball court practicing shots and ball handling. Over time, I got better.

Nevertheless, I realized that even with hard work, I would never be able to catch up to my friends as soon as I wanted to because they had far too many years of experience on me. I was shocked when I shot two air balls in a row one day and they did not make fun of me. Instead, one of them slapped me on the back, wished me better luck next time, and told me to run to the other side of the court. I realized then that they had begun to respect me because I had taken the time to understand the game. They became skilled because they valued basketball as an art and had sacrificed much of their time to the game. As I continue to work hard, I will not only shoot fewer air balls, but will also develop a further appreciation of the game that will help me become a better player overall.

7. Why did you pick your major and/or what are your life goals?

This question asks you to:

i.   Describe which academic subjects interest you.

ii.   Explain why these academic subjects interest you.

iii.   Explain how these academic subjects relate to your career and life goals.

iv.   Relate your specific intellectual curiosities and goals to what the school you are applying to can offer you.

This question does not ask you to:

i.   Talk about being able to choose your major after taking classes and then state that you will not change your major even if you explore other classes.

ii.   Talk about superficial goals of making more money or being powerful as reasons for choosing your major.

iii.   Use your parents as the sole reason for why you are applying to your specific major or have specific life goals.

Most Asian students apply as Business/Economics, Math and Science-type majors. Business and Economics are popular majors at most American universities, so choosing this major will probably not make an Asian candidate more competitive. Choosing Math and some Sciences will make Asian students more competitive.

Despite a common trend among the majors of Asian applicants, most students still have trouble writing a good essay about why they have chosen their major. Most students begin this paragraph with an exclamation that they are excited about American universities because it is an opportunity to explore the liberal arts. Two sentences later, they negate their first comment to state that regardless of the benefit of being able to take classes and then choose their major, they will not wait and will in fact actually choose Economics or Engineering anyway. This is not a good way to write this essay and admissions readers are not impressed by it. It is better when students say they want to take advantage of the liberal arts atmosphere by taking various Literature, Math, and Economics classes and then confirm their major.

Students often incorrectly list money and power as two key reasons for choosing their major. American universities do not like this approach. Another way of phrasing "make money and be powerful" is "make an impact/a difference in society/the world". This approach works much better and presents a humbler attitude. Again, be very careful when trying to use money, power or prestige as a reason for choosing a major or career path.

Acing the App

My favorite "why my major" essay to date was one written by a student on film. She had a real passion for the subject. She did not want to apply to the University of Southern California (USC) because she wanted to become the next famous director. Instead, she wanted to refine her techniques, learn from others, benefit from the Los Angeles cinema atmosphere, and develop as an artist. With guidance, she wrote a great essay. Passion for a subject is an uncommon theme among application essays written by mainland Chinese students; however, it can be greatly beneficial to those who execute it appropriately.

As noted earlier, many students write that they want to choose a given career path because of parental pressure or because they want to follow in their parents' footsteps. This type of reason requires a very tricky explanation that students often mess up. Be careful when taking this approach. Make sure to emphasize that you esteem and admire your parents for their work. Also include that because your parents are in the same line of work you hope to pursue, you have insight into the field, and that has already confirmed your interest.

See examples below of what to write and what not to write.

Example:

Born in a family with father pursuing Chemistry-related business, I have been cultivated a good sense of chemical learning since my childhood. Thus I could have a dream that one day I could enter a real fascinating laboratory, holding test tubes and wearing protection glasses.

Actually I first developed an interest in Chemistry in hospital with mother taking responsibility of chemical examinations. That was the first place I saw many bottles of different sizes and I even had not idea of the exact names. Looking at the bubbles coming out of the bottom of a measuring cup, I was thinking about the explicit process of the chemical reaction.

I have been always amazed by things beyond regular cognitive measures of human, from high-resolution images through microscope to occurrence on planets in outer space. Hence I always stare at the transparent containers for a chemical guess. High school education of Chemistry concentrates on giving students a solid ground of various elements and their characteristics. However, I could not access to "how" and "why" which then turned to motivate me for a grounded learning.

Possibly I might not be able to handle complicated questions but clearly I know what kind of expertise that Chemistry demands. Though Chemistry in classroom loses some of its original enticements if being separated from experiments, I still closely followed every point of teacher's articulation, and cherished and seized every chance in experiment class to test and see, then I could think and digest a chemical formula and carry on accurate calculations. I also know Chemistry is a highly integrated discipline with daily life. As early as Chemistry was offered in junior high, I would find anything possible to imitate laboratory operations at home. Constantly a basin would be the reaction container, wires would work for electrodes. Despite of failures more than successes, I founded a life interest with an early take-off as the start of a career.

Notes on the essay:

The student presents a complete picture of why he or she has a passion for Chemistry. However, I have seen this type of explanation (my parents are in the field, I like this specifically, and I hope to do more in college with regards to Chemistry) many, many times. The above essay would be okay for a lower ranked school, but if students want to stand out, they should try to imagine unique ways of presenting their interest in Chemistry.

Better example:

Big pyramids. Usually when one thinks of Egypt, the first thought on one's mind is the great pyramids. However, as a child, I fell in love with Egypt for a different reason. I found it fascinating that they used natural resources to produce pigments for adding intense eye makeup and also understood how to best utilize plants to make products ranging from cheese, soap, bronze and even medicine. Since my father's career centered on Chemistry, he pointed out these intricate processes to me at an early age. The Egyptians looked like magicians to me. They could add two elements and create something entirely different from them. At that age, I had no idea that the Egyptians had begun to lay the foundation for basic Chemistry.

Later, my mother introduced me to hospital laboratories. This was my first interaction with modern Chemistry. I found these bottles with their slowly revolving liquid centers as fascinating as the programs I had previously watched on television about the

Acing the App

Egyptians. I began to believe that perhaps one day I would cure diseases as the Egyptians had. The only difference would be that I would hold test tubes instead of solely plants and I would wear protective glasses and a lab coat instead of a loincloth.

Right now I am taking Chemistry in high school. Every day I race to class excited to learn more about my favorite topic. I learn how to manipulate chemicals to create reactions in the lab. I have learned to appreciate atoms for what they are. I see the world and the objects within them in terms of their chemical makeup. In a world where new elements are synthesized and products are full of unhealthy substances, I am interested in pursuing a degree that will help me best understand the properties of medicine derived from natural sources. For this reason, I must study Pharmacognosy. I have read many works by The American Society of Pharmacognosy and it is my belief that through this interpretation of Chemistry I will best manifest my childhood dreams. I also want to learn German in college because it is my dream to one day work at BASF, the biggest chemical company in the world. With the type of education and internship opportunities offered at your school, I know that I would be able to accomplish my goals.

9. Essay Tutorials

This chapter will help you brainstorm and write responses to the most common essay prompts. For each prompt, there are six sections: questions, brainstorming, content summary, writing the essay, reviewing the essay, and rewriting the essay. Remember that admissions readers will judge you according to your essay, so use these six parts to write the best essay you can.

- **Questions:** I have written a set of questions that you should ask yourself as you begin to write.

- **Brainstorming:** Answering the questions from the previous section here will help you think about possible prompt response topics. You will also see that some questions are repeated in multiple prompts. This will allow you to copy some of what you have written from one area to another.

- **Content summary:** Afterwards, you will summarize the most important information from the brainstorming section here.

- **Writing the essay:** You will then use the information from the summary section to write your response in this part.

- **Reviewing the essay:** When you get to this section, ask a friend, counselor or native English speaker to correct your previous part using a red pen and leave comments for you in this section. It is very important that someone else gives you feedback on your work because often times we miss our mistakes when we review our own work.

- **Rewriting the essay:** Later, fix your mistakes and improve your writing in this section. Rewrite as many times as you want. I would encourage rewriting your essay at least once.

1. Describe an activity that you have participated in.

Questions:

- Write a list of your activities.

- In which of these have you had a leadership position? Write those positions.

- In which of these have you had an interesting experience? Could this experience be fashioned into a story that represents positive qualities about you? What is that story? What are the positive qualities? What do these qualities say about you as a person?

- Why do you like this activity?

- Have you had an internship, conducted research or worked? If so, with whom or for what company? What did you do? What did you learn? How did you grow?

Brainstorming:

_____

_____

_____

_____

_____

_____

_____

_____

_____

_____

Acing the App

Content summary:

_____
_____
_____
_____
_____
_____
_____
_____
_____

Writing the essay:

_____
_____
_____
_____
_____
_____
_____
_____
_____

Reviewing the essay:

_____
_____
_____
_____
_____
_____
_____
_____
_____
_____

Rewriting the essay:

_____

_____

_____

_____

_____

_____

_____

_____

_____

2. Tell us about where you come from and how this has shaped who you are.

Questions:

- Where were you born? Where is your hometown? Does your hometown have special customs? What defines your culture? Do you feel this has impacted you?

- Are you religious? Has this community shaped you in some way that you think makes you different and unique from the majority of applicants?

- If you are Chinese, are you an ethnic minority? Are you part of the Han majority? Has this affected you in any way? What does your ethnicity say about you as a Chinese person?

- Are you male or female? Has being your gender affected you in any way, shape or form?

- Are you part of a sports team or an academic team? What is your position on the team? Do you like this activity? What have you learned from your teammates?

- What events (as part of any of the above communities) shaped who you are?

- Have you experienced any life-changing events? Has one event made you act differently?

Acing the App

Brainstorming:

_____
_____
_____
_____
_____
_____
_____
_____

Content summary:

_____
_____
_____
_____
_____
_____
_____
_____

Writing the essay:

_____
_____
_____
_____
_____
_____
_____
_____
_____

Reviewing the essay:

_____

_____

_____

_____

_____

_____

_____

_____

_____

Rewriting the essay:

_____

_____

_____

_____

_____

_____

_____

_____

_____

3. Talk about an experience.

Questions:

- Of all the events in your life, is there one experience that stands out to you?

- Is there an event in your life that has helped you decide a major, find a new interest or pursue a career path? If so, discuss and talk about how it made you change your mind.

- Has there been a person in your life who has greatly affected you? Did you meet a friend who taught you a lot about the world? Did the death of a grandparent or another loved one teach you something? How have you grown from it?

Acing the App

Brainstorming:

_____
_____
_____
_____
_____
_____
_____
_____
_____

Content summary:

_____
_____
_____
_____
_____
_____
_____
_____

Writing the essay:

_____
_____
_____
_____
_____
_____
_____
_____
_____

Reviewing the essay:

_____

_____

_____

_____

_____

_____

_____

_____

_____

Rewriting the essay:

_____

_____

_____

_____

_____

_____

_____

_____

_____

4. Why do you want to apply to X school?

Questions:

- What major or majors are you considering?

- Does this school have good programs in your major(s)? If yes, why are they special?

- Does this school have good resources for your major(s)? If yes, why are these resources specific and special to this school? How are these resources different from those offered at other schools?

- What are the special courses offered in your major(s)?

Acing the App

- Are there renowned professors you can conduct research alongside? What are their names? What are their areas of research? What classes do they teach?

- What minors does the school have that you are interested in?

- Does the school have any certificate programs you want to complete?

- What special orientation programs does this school have?

- What are your hobbies? Does this school have clubs to support your hobbies?

- Do you want to join new groups? Does this school have any clubs you want to join?

- Where is this school located? Do you like the location? What specifically do you like about the location?

- Did you visit the school? What did you like best about it?

- What is the school's motto? Does it align with your educational goals?

- If you are not an American, why do you want to apply to schools in the United States? How are American universities different from your home country's universities?

- If you are not an American, how can you benefit from attending a university in the United States instead of your home country?

- Do you have any friends at the school? If so, what have they told you about the school that makes you like it?

Brainstorming:

_____

_____

_____

_____

_____

_____

_____

_____

_____

Content summary:

_____

_____

_____

_____

_____

_____

_____

_____

_____

Writing the essay:

_____

_____

_____

_____

_____

_____

_____

_____

_____

Reviewing the essay:

_____

_____

_____

_____

_____

_____

_____

_____

_____

Acing the App

Rewriting the essay:

_____

_____

_____

_____

_____

_____

_____

_____

_____

5. What are you most proud of? What does this say about you?

Questions:

- Are you especially proud of one of your accomplishments?

- Are you dedicated, honest, committed, etc.? Are you proud of being this way?

- Why is this important in your life? How did you become like this? What does it say about your potential?

- Have you ever faced a moral dilemma? How did you respond? What does this say about who you are?

Brainstorming:

_____

_____

_____

_____

_____

_____

_____

_____

_____

Content summary:

_____

_____

_____

_____

_____

_____

_____

_____

_____

Writing the essay:

_____

_____

_____

_____

_____

_____

_____

_____

_____

_____

Reviewing the essay:

_____

_____

_____

_____

_____

_____

_____

_____

_____

Acing the App

Rewriting the essay:

_____

_____

_____

_____

_____

_____

_____

_____

_____

_____

6. What obstacles have you faced and what does overcoming these obstacles say about you?

Questions:

- Have you ever faced a moral dilemma? How did you respond? What does this say about who you are?

- Did you ever have trouble with a class or an assignment? How did It feel? How did you try to fix the situation?

- Have you suffered from a tragedy, overcame it and learned a lot in the process? What was your tragedy? What did you do to overcome it? What did you learn?

Brainstorming:

_____

_____

_____

_____

_____

_____

_____

_____

_____

Content summary:

_____

_____

_____

_____

_____

_____

_____

_____

_____

Writing the essay:

_____

_____

_____

_____

_____

_____

_____

_____

_____

Reviewing the essay:

_____

_____

_____

_____

_____

_____

_____

_____

Acing the App

Rewriting the essay:

_____

_____

_____

_____

_____

_____

_____

_____

7. Why did you pick your major and/or what are your life goals?

Questions:

- What are you passionate about?

- What major or majors are you considering? Why are you interested in majoring in them? What life experience have you had that makes you want to dedicate four years of study to the major(s)?

- Does this school have good programs in your major(s)? If yes, why are they special?

- Does this school have good resources for your major(s)? If yes, why are these resources specific and special to this school? How are these resources different from those offered at other schools?

- What are the special courses offered in your major(s)?

- Are there renowned professors you can conduct research alongside? What are their names? What are their areas of research? What classes do they teach?

- What minors does the school have that you are interested in?

- Does the school have any certificate programs you want to complete?

- Will the location of this school help you achieve your goals in some way? (For example, an Environmental Studies major picks a school next to an environmental sanctuary or nature conservatory. An Economics major picks a school in New York because it is the world's finance capital.)

Brainstorming:

_____

_____

_____

_____

_____

_____

_____

_____

_____

Content summary:

_____

_____

_____

_____

_____

_____

_____

_____

_____

Writing the essay:

_____

_____

_____

_____

_____

_____

_____

_____

_____

Acing the App

Reviewing the essay:

_____

_____

_____

_____

_____

_____

_____

_____

_____

Rewriting the essay:

_____

_____

_____

_____

_____

_____

_____

_____

_____

10. Writing the Resume and Filling Out the Activities Form

Writing a resume is one of the most important parts of completing a good college application. While some colleges ask for an activities form, it is always good to have a resume on hand. If you have an extensive activities list, you should even send your one-page resume to schools through regular mail or attach it as a document to your Common App supplemental sections if allowed.

Your resume should highlight your extra-curricular activities, internships, awards and volunteer experiences. Generally speaking, your resume should only mention what happened in what is your equivalent of the four years of American high school (all of senior middle school and the third year of junior middle school if attending mainland Chinese schools). Colleges believe that the most important information on resumes will have occurred during this time period. Although there are rare exceptions, you should almost never include something from before freshman year (the third year of junior middle school if in a mainland Chinese school). It does not impress admissions officers to see a list of accomplishments from age four onward. Rather, including this information detracts from your overall application.

In the United States, resume and curriculum vitae (CV) lengths for high school and college students should not exceed one page. Although you may feel like you have a lot to write about, I guarantee you that there is a way to get everything that is important down to only one page. When writing about activities, do not simply list your duties as part of that organization. Instead, it is important to list accomplishments and numbers. When writing about your activities, you should always use ACTION verbs. Examples of both how to describe activities and what action verbs are will follow this section.

The titles you use in your resume are very important. These titles draw attention to your strengths. For example, if you do not have any work experience, do not list that section. If you have a lot of music experience, perhaps list that as an entire section.

Resume Section Titles List

The following is a list of titles for possible sections on your resume. Categorizing your resume like this will help you fill out an activities form faster and will impress admissions officers when you do send them your resume. When reviewing this list, note that you do not have to and should not include all of these titles on your resume; they are just suggestions.

- Education
- Activities/Extra-Curricular Involvement
- Leadership Experience
- International Experience
- Program Experience
- Conferences Attended
- Work Experience
- Professional Experience
- Volunteer Experience
- Music Experience

- Artistic Experience

- Skills (Does not include hobbies or interests, which is a common mistake mainland Chinese students make)

- Hobbies/Interests (Very different from skills)

- Languages (If you speak languages besides English and your native language)

- Awards

In working with mainland Chinese students, I have noticed a pattern in activities. Students from other Asian countries may notice a similar pattern. The following activities are the most common activities I have come across:

- Model United Nations

- Student Government

- Sports Teams

- Olympic Activities Volunteer

- Volunteer in poor and underprivileged areas, especially as an English teacher

- Recycling to raise money

- 班长 *(Banzhang)* and/or 课代表 *(Kedaibiao)*

Since these are the most common examples I have come across, I have decided to give examples of how you can write about each one of these points in your resume below.

The EDUCATION Section of a Resume

The first section of a high school or college level resume should always be EDUCATION. The education section will at minimum include the names of your junior middle school and senior middle school in addition to the years attended. If your Grade Point Average (GPA) is strong at either or both levels, this can be included after the school names. You can also list your class rank instead of GPA. To an American admissions officer, rank may be a better indicator of your success in the class than GPA since they may not understand your transcript entirely. You can also use this section to highlight your TOEFL, SAT and other scores. I have included an example of this in the Sample Resume section. See below for a basic format of how to include your education information. Everything in brackets is optional.

> *Education*
> Name of High School, Diploma Expected YEAR (GPA)
> (Rank)
> (TOEFL or IELTS) (SAT I)
> (SAT II) (SAT II) (SAT II)

> Example 1:
> *Education*
> Qingdao Star High School, Diploma Expected 20XX, GPA: 4.8
> TOEFL: 96 SAT I: 1980

> Example 2:
> *Education*
> Kunming Senior Middle School 2, Diploma Expected 20XX
> Rank: 3 out of 300
> TOEFL: 100 SAT I: 2100
> SAT II Math: 800 SAT II Chemistry: 780

What is an EXTRA-CURRICULAR ACTIVITY?

An EXTRA-CURRICULAR ACTIVITY is any activity that a student does in addition to academics. These include but are not limited to: Model United Nations, volunteer groups, Math Club, Science Club, student government, internships, etc. Depending on the number of activities you have of any one kind, they can also form their own heading on your resume. For example, if you only participated in one volunteer organization, you could list that in your extra-curricular activities section. However, if you participated in four or five different kinds, you should create a special section called Volunteer Experience.

Acing the App

Some Asian international students lack extensive extra-curricular activities because they grow up in an educational system focused solely on testing. These students can set themselves apart from their peers by engaging in extra-curricular activities outside the classroom from an early age. American colleges especially admire students who have held leadership roles in their extra-curricular activities.

The basic format for listing an activity is as follows.

NAME OF ORGANIZATION, Position(s): Dates Involved

- Accomplishments as part of this organization AND/OR

- Responsibilities as a part of this organization

Examples:

Model United Nations, Moderator: May 20XX to Present

- Oversaw a team of 30 people

- Led team to the Shenzhen Championship (1st place out of 30 teams)

- Helped organize the first overseas Model United Nations trip at my school

Student Government, Treasurer: August 20XX to Present

- Oversaw the financials for all Student Government activities

- Managed a yearly activities fund of 10,000 CNY

What is WORK EXPERIENCE?

WORK EXPERIENCE includes any internships or real jobs a student has held. This can include working at a family member's company during summer vacation, interning with a local company, working at a restaurant, etc.

The basic format for listing work experience or internship experience (both titles can be used depending on your experience) is as follows.

NAME OF COMPANY, Position: Dates Involved

- Accomplishments AND/OR

- Duties included

Examples:

L Computers, Summer Intern: July 20XX

- Wrote reports that summarized pros and cons of certain types of computers

- Presented a major report to the management head on findings

Northeastern Chinese Bank: August 20XX

- Reviewed statistical data to improve bank procedures

- Attended management meetings to learn about the inner workings of a bank

What is **VOLUNTEER EXPERIENCE?**

VOLUNTEER EXPERIENCE includes activities in which you do something to assist a disadvantaged group or something to protect the environment. Assisting at a senior citizens' home, fundraising for a cause, tutoring or recycling can be included in this category.

The basic format for listing a volunteer activity is as follows.

NAME OF ACTIVITY/VOLUNTEER GROUP, Position: Dates Involved

- Duties included AND/OR

- Accomplishments (If any)

Examples:

Aihao Senior Citizen Home, Volunteer: May 20XX to Present

- Assisted senior citizens with daily activities

- Donated 7,000 CNY to build better facilities

OR (You would not list the activity twice. You should either list it as shown above or as shown below. The example above describes the student's activity as part of the club over time. The example below only mentions the student's participation in the event We Care Aihao.)

We Care Aihao, Leader: May 2011

- Raised 7,000 CNY to donate to Aihao Senior Citizen Home

Acing the App

Helping Hand, Member: April 2011 to Present

- Tutored 10th and 11th grade students in Math

What Kinds Of PROGRAMS/CONFERENCES Do I List?

If you have attended programs and conferences, these should be included on your resume. This is not usually something that you can list on an activities form, but is something that is acceptable and encouraged on a resume. Admissions officers like to see that students have attended programs or conferences. It shows that students are invested in their education. Different types of programs and conferences can be included here. If you have attended a summer school program at an American university, list it here. If you have attended special conferences for Model United Nations or a special program to help you debate better, list that. If you have attended a conference on a specific topic, such as Biology or Psychology, definitely list it.

If you won an award at one of these conferences or programs, you should list it under the awards section; not here, unless you are not including an awards section on your resume.

The basic format for listing a program or conference is as follows.

NAME OF PROGRAM/CONFERENCE, Dates: Location

Examples:

Beijing Psychology in the 21st Century Conference, June 20XX: Beijing

Young Scholars Program, January 20XX: Sichuan

What Kinds Of AWARDS Do I List?

AWARDS from the past four years should be listed. This can include awards given at school and awards given outside of school. If the meaning of an award may be unclear to admissions officers, you may define it.

The basic format for listing an award is as follows.

AWARD [Explanation], Date Received

Examples:

1st Place, Math Competition, April 20XX

Bright Scholar Award of China: An award given to the top student in their class during the 11th grade, July 20XX

Honorable Mention: Model United Nations Beijing Conference, March 20XX

ACTION Verbs

When writing resumes in English, students must remember to use ACTION verbs to describe their activities. It is better to use action verbs because they are more dynamic and lend themselves to leader-oriented sentences. As a general rule, action verbs should be in the past tense If you're no longer doing them and the present tense if you are still in the process of doing that.

Several great actions verbs can be found below.

- Assisted with
- Organized

- Donated
- Oversaw

- Elected
- Programmed

- Learned
- Raised

- Led
- Trained

- Managed

Examples:
- Organized a workshop to improve laboratory skills

- Managed a conference for over 500 students

- Donated 7,500 CNY to Aihao Charity

How to Explain 班长 (*Banzhang*) or 课代表 (*Kedaibiao*)

For a mainland Chinese student, explaining the role of a *Banzhang* or *Kedaibiao* is a common problem when applying to college. Most American high schools lack an equivalent position so when college admissions readers see this title on an application, most do not immediately know what to think about it. Responsibilities can also vary from school to school. Since *Banzhang* and *Kedaibiao* are essential leadership positions, students should do their best to accurately describe them.

If you are including *Banzhang* or *Kedaibiao* in your activities list on The Common App but not in your personal statement or supplemental essays, you may want to use the additional information section of The Common App to describe what exactly a *Banzhang* or *Kedaibiao* is.

Below are several ways to explain *Banzhang* and *Kedaibiao*.

- *Banzhang* is a special honor given to one person per classroom. The *Banzhang* is similar to a model, guide or leader within the class rather than a reporter or monitor. The *Banzhang* is responsible for maintaining order in a class by facilitating self-study classes, collecting fees, and communicating as the student body representative of that class to the school administration.

- A *Banzhang* is head of the entire class; a *Kedaibiao* is the head student of a particular subject.

- The *Kedaibiao* is responsible for all academic issues related to a subject. In China, these teacher assistants are very important. The class cannot run without them. The *Kedaibiao* often grade papers, collect homework, record missing assignments, and hear academic suggestions.

A resume can make specific reference to how many students the *Banzhang* or *Kedaibiao* oversaw in addition to specific duties performed.

Sample Resume

Below you will find a sample resume and an area for you to fill in your own information. Look at the sample resume to see what a good resume looks like.

Name of Student

Address * Phone Number * Email

Education

Harbin High School, Diploma Expected June 20XX

Rank: 2 out of 400 students

TOEFL Score: 104 Highest SAT Combined: 2100

SAT II Biology-M: 700 SAT II Math IIC: 750 SAT II History: 650

Work Experience

Blank Company: Intern, August 20XX

Organized mini-workshops every week to increase productivity among workers

Interviewed senior managers in order to learn more about each department and make a more thorough assessment of the business during my time there

Created slideshow presentations in both Chinese and English for a workshop on brand positioning

Leadership Experience

Student Government: Elected Class Vice-President, 20XX–20XX

Debated resolutions to improve school safety and cafeteria sanitation

Organized speech contests, drama competitions, debate competitions, etc.

Words Speak: Co-Founder and Editor-in-Chief, 20XX

Oversaw content and edited articles for the newspaper

Average of 500 copies sold per issue

Sichuan Earthquake Relief Fund: Main Coordinator, October 20XX

Organized a silent auction and bottle collecting drive to raise money for victims of the Sichuan Earthquake

Raised XX,XXX CNY (Approximately X,XXX USD)

Conferences and Programs Attended

Fudan Conference on Behavioral Neuroscience, Shanghai, China: Conference Participant, August 20XX

Global Youth Leadership Conference (GYLC), Boston, USA: Selected Representative, July 20XX

Summer Model United Nations Camp at Brown University, Rhode Island, USA: Student Participant, July 20XX

Awards and Honors

Chinese Patent Number XXXXXX, Issued July 21, 20XX

Straight A Student Award, Received May 20XX

Beijing Normal Poetry Contest: 1st Place, Received April 20XX

Xinjiang Pianist Contest: 2nd Place, Received January 20XX

What is an Activities Form?

An activities form is used by colleges to measure a student's level of involvement in their high school and potential involvement in their college. An activities form often includes the following categories which students are expected to fill out.

- Type of activity

- Leadership positions held (If any)

- Honors or Awards (If any)

- Employer (For employment experience or internships)

- Grades participated (9th = 3rd year junior middle school, 10th = 1st year senior middle school, 11th = 2nd year senior middle school, 12th = 3rd year senior middle school)

- Time of activity (During school time or during a school break, for example, in the summer)

- Hours per week and weeks per year

- Description of duties and/or accomplishments (This ranges anywhere from one line to a few sentences)

If you write a resume, it will be easy to transfer this information to an activities form.

Resume Form

Fill in your resume and then type up the information below to make it look like the sample resume.

(Write your name in bigger font with your address, phone number and email address below it in smaller font.)

_____

Education (Insert the name of your high school and the diploma expected date.)

_____

Rank: _____

TOEFL Score: _____ Highest SAT Combined: _____

SAT II Subject: _____ SAT II Subject: _____ SAT II Subject: _____

_____ **Experience** (Insert your first type of experience here. Describe different activities or internships that fall under this type of experience and use a numbered section for each involvement. Do not include the number when you type it up.)

1. _____

_____

_____

_____

_____

Acing the App

_____

_____

_____

_____

_____

2. _____

_____

_____

_____

_____

_____

_____

_____

3. _____

_____

_____

_____

_____

_____

_____

_____

_____

_____

_____ **Experience** (Insert your second type of experience here. Describe different activities or internships that fall under this type of experience and use a numbered section for each involvement. Do not include the number when you type it up.)

1. _____

_____

_____

_____

_____

_____

_____

_____

_____

_____

2. _____

_____

_____

_____

_____

_____

_____

_____

_____

_____

3. _____

_____

_____

_____

_____

_____

Acing the App

_____

_____

_____

_____

_____ **Experience** (Insert your third type of experience here. Describe different activities or internships that fall under this type of experience and use a numbered section for each involvement. Do not include the number when you type it up.)

1. _____

_____

_____

_____

_____

_____

_____

_____

2. _____

_____

_____

_____

_____

_____

_____

_____

_____

3. _____

_____

_____

_____

_____

_____

_____

_____

_____ **Attended** (Insert conferences and programs attended. Include locations, dates and the capacity in which you attended. Do not include the numbers when you type this section.)

1. _____

2. _____

3. _____

4. _____

Awards and Honors (Insert your awards and honors below. Include dates received. Do not include the numbers when you type this section.)

1. _____

2. _____

3. _____

4. _____

Use the space below to write anything you could not fit in the above sections.

_____

_____

_____

_____

_____

_____

_____

_____

_____

_____

11. Letters of Recommendation

Letters of Recommendation (also known as Recommendation Letters and RLs) are a VERY important part of the application process for American schools. They should come from teachers who know you well. My students sometimes have a hard time believing this but American universities rather receive a recommendation letter from someone who knows you well and can write a lot about you than from someone who is important at your school but barely knows you. You are a more competitive candidate if only teachers who know you well write your recommendation letters. Again, at the undergraduate level, American schools do not care about the seniority of the person writing your recommendation letter. They place more emphasis on that person's ability to give detailed, helpful information about you.

Best Tactics for Writing a Good Recommendation Letter

It is much harder to find a teacher who is willing to write a recommendation letter for you in China and other Asian countries than in the United States. Below are the possible scenarios you will face with regards to recommendation letters.

- *Best possible scenario:* Give the following questions to your teacher and have him or her fill it out in the form of a recommendation letter in your native language (unless he or she can write English well). You or someone else should translate the letter from your native language to English. American universities appreciate seeing the original copy and the English translation. If you have an official notary stamp certifying the translation, that is even better!

- *Next scenario:* Give the following questions to your teacher and have him or her respond to these questions in your native language (or English if he or she can speak English well). Format these responses into a recommendation letter yourself. Show it to your teacher and ask for suggestions. Translate this letter from your native language to English. American universities appreciate seeing the original copy and the English translation. If you have an official notary stamp certifying the translation, that is even better!

- *Worst case scenario:* In the United States, some teachers and professors agree to sign recommendation letters for their students if the students themselves will write the letter. Students may sometimes run into this problem. In this instance, students should do the following:

  - Use the questions in the following section.

  - Respond to the questions as you think your teacher would respond.

  - Show your written responses to your teacher. Ask him or her for suggestions if he or she is willing to give them.

  - Turn these responses into a recommendation letter.

  - Give your teacher the final letter to review and have him or her sign it.

  - Translate the letter from your native language to English if this teacher Is not a native English speaker.

- *What students sometimes do, but should not:* Sometimes students pay agencies to write their recommendation letters. American colleges are getting better and better at figuring out which recommendation letters are written this way. I always advise my students that in the event the teachers cannot write the letters, they should at least have some involvement. Personal experience with and anecdotes about the student are very important parts of the recommendation letter. Most American colleges can tell when a recommendation letter lacks substance because someone who does not know the student in an academic capacity wrote it. For top 30 schools that require recommendation letters, it is important to include good references as part of your application. For schools below top 30, recommendation letters are generally not as important as other parts of your application.

Questions to Answer in a Recommendation Letter

1. How long have you known the student and in what capacity?

2. What adjectives would you use to describe the student?

3. Give two examples from your experience with the student that shows he or she is a good student and would contribute as a student to X University.

4. How does what you know about the student relate to his or her intended major and/or career path?

5. Is there any additional information that we should know about this student?

6. How would you sum up this student in one sentence?

7. If you speak English and are willing to have an admissions officer speak to you on behalf of the student, please write yes here.

8. What is your full name, title, work address, work email address, and work phone number?

Teachers or students can use the above questions to fill out a form that will help structure a recommendation letter. Examples of a fill-in question form and a fill-in recommendation letter form can be found at the end of this chapter.

Do's and Don'ts

Do's

- Once the full name of the student is introduced in the first sentence, he or she should only be referred to by either their first name or Ms./Mr. LAST NAME for the rest of the recommendation letter.

- Only state how long or since when you have known the student once. I have often seen the beginning of recommendation letters state the same fact multiple times. The following is an example of what I usually see: "I have known X student for three years when they first took my English class. Since 20XX when the student enrolled, I knew X would be a great student." Only one sentence is necessary.

- Write "X student has deeply impressed me" or "X is an impressive student". I have seen many letters where recommenders write "gave me a deep impression". This is not a correct statement in English, but it can be easily corrected by following this advice.

- Write about the student's strong character outside of the classroom. For instance, one student's recommendation letter translated to: "In my opinion, X's unwavering devotion to his community exemplifies strong moral fiber and character. He is a trustworthy individual and would be an excellent candidate for your school."

- Show that the student is different from his or her peers, for example: "Unlike other interns who were wearing T-shirts, X was dressed in a formal suit."

- Use other words besides "greedy". I have seen many recommendation translations and originals use the phrase "X student is a greedy learner". "Greedy" has a negative connotation in English and should not be used. Instead, one can write "X student has a healthy/insatiable intellectual appetite". It has more or less the same meaning, but without a negative connotation.

- Try to minimize mix-ups using he and she or him and her. He and him are used for males. She and her are used for females. This can make an otherwise good recommendation letter annoying to an admissions reader. One mishap is not an issue, but if it is prevalent throughout the essay, it could be detrimental.

Acing the App

Don'ts

- I have come across recommendation letters that flaunt a student's connections. Contrary to popular opinion in several Asian countries, these types of recommendation letters make a student less likely to get into an American university. American colleges prefer to think that a student is worthy on his or her own account and not due to family connections. Schools will learn about a student's family through the parent information section on most applications. You can explain your family's importance in this section if you like.

- I have seen some recommendation letters include skills such as "sitting and reading books" or "does their homework". American students are expected to be able to do these things. Writing these as examples can detract from a student's overall application.

- I have seen many recommendation letters describe high school and university students as "promising young girl" or "promising young boy". Although these students are still young, it is better to refer to them as "promising young woman" or "promising young man".

The Fill-In Question Form Example

I will be using the examples of Mr. Han and Ms. Wang to show how to use the forms below.

1. How long have you known the student and in what capacity?

   a. Mr. Han: Two years; Chemistry teacher

   b. Ms. Wang: Three years; Traditional Chinese Literature teacher

2. What adjectives would you use to describe the student?

   a. Mr. Han: Hardworking, self-motivated, pleasant

   b. Ms. Wang: Bright, curious, dedicated

3. Give two examples from your experience with the student that shows he or she is a good student and would contribute as a student to X University.

   a. Mr. Han: Tutoring another student, had trouble understanding oxidation and reduction

   b. Ms. Wang: *Dream of the Red Chamber* play, highest test scores/study charts

4. How does what you know about the student relate to his or her intended major and/or career path?

   a. Mr. Han: Chemistry major, doctor

   b. Ms. Wang: Undecided major, open career path

5. Is there any additional information that we should know about this student?

   a. Mr. Han: Volunteers at a nearby clinic

   b. Ms. Wang: Nothing to add (This section will be left out.)

6. How would you sum up this student in one sentence?

   a. Mr. Han: Mr. Han is a dedicated young man who will definitely make an excellent student at your university.

   b. Ms. Wang: Ms. Wang is a bright, young woman with unlimited potential, and will benefit from and contribute to your university.

7. If you speak English and are willing to have an admissions officer speak to you on behalf of the student, please write yes here.

   a. Mr. Han: (Left blank. This section will be left out.)

   b. Ms. Wang: Yes

8. What is your full name, title, work address, work email address, and work phone number?

   a. Mr. Han: Han Zhi, Chemistry Teacher, ADDRESS, hz@123.com, +86 145-203-234X

   b. Ms. Wang: Jia Tang, Literature Teacher & Assistant Counselor, ADDRESS, jt1352@123.com, +86 145-203-234X

Acing the App

Using the Fill-In Question Form

1. How long have you known the student and in what capacity?

How to answer #1: When answering this question, teachers will most likely write the number of years and in what way they know the student, such as a teacher, counselor, principal, etc. There are two main ways you can turn this information into a sentence that can be useful in the recommendation letter. Both of these are listed below.

    a. Mr. Han: Two years; Chemistry teacher

        i. Sentence: I have known Mr. Han for two years. I first met him when he enrolled in my Chemistry class.

    b. Ms. Wang: Three years; Traditional Chinese Literature teacher

        i. Sentence: I have known Ms. Wang since 2008 when she first took my Traditional Chinese Literature course.

2. What adjectives would you use to describe the student?

How to use #2: Key, meaningful adjectives about the student should be used in the introductory paragraph. All adjectives can be used in one sentence (example a) or elaborated upon in multiple sentences by giving reasons for why you think the student exhibits these characteristics (example b).

    a. Mr. Han: Hardworking, self-motivated, pleasant

        i. Sentence: Mr. Han is an extremely hardworking student, a self-motivator and a pleasure to have in class.

    b. Ms. Wang: Bright, curious, dedication

        i. Sentence: Ms. Wang is an exceptionally bright student. She has a unique curiosity of the world that is apparent in the multitude of questions that she asks during class. I believe this curiosity helps fuel her dedication to learning. Because she wants to learn as much as possible, she works very hard to memorize all the information and then analyze it in order to be able to better contribute to class discussions.

3. Give two examples from your experience with the student that shows he or she is a good student and would contribute as a student to X University.

How to use #3: Anecdotes should be described in moderate detail and should mention how the characteristics described will contribute to the student being a good university student.

a. Mr. Han: Tutoring another student, had trouble understanding oxidation and reduction

i. Paragraph 1: Mr. Han is an exemplary student who not only thinks of himself but also of his fellow classmates. Since Mr. Han has extraordinary skills of memorization, he received a flawless score on our periodic table exam. On the other hand, he noticed that two of his peers had not found it as easy. Since their scores were so low, he petitioned me to give them extra credit points to count towards their score if they could get full marks on a makeup test. I allowed it and watched Mr. Han spend every lunch break and two hours after school each day for a week practicing with them. In the end, both students received perfect scores. Mr. Han has assisted his classmates in a similar fashion on two other occasions.

ii. Paragraph 2: Not only does Mr. Han know how to lead his classmates and give them a helping hand, Mr. Han also knows how to ask for help when he needs it. One day after a second lesson on oxidation and reduction reactions, Mr. Han approached me to tell me that he had been having trouble understanding the equations. He came back every day during lunch until the test date and worked on additional problems with me. By the time the test came around, he did well. I believe that this experience is an example of Mr. Han being proactive. He did not wait until he had a bad test score, but rather immediately recognized that he was having trouble and sought help.

b. Ms. Wang: *Dream of the Red Chamber* play, highest test scores/study charts

i. Paragraph 1: In China, almost all high schools teach *Dream of the Red Chamber*, a classic Chinese novel. Every year, students write me wonderful papers on themes of a male-dominated society and feudalism in China. Ms. Wang's ten-page essay on the role of women during the Qing dynasty via this novel impressed me and is among one of the best papers I have ever read. Her interpretation of the 12 beauties of Jinling surprised me. I made copies of the essay with comments and without her name. I then passed it out to the class. In this way, my students were able to see a peer example of a good paper and be exposed to the ideas of Ms. Wang.

    ii. Paragraph 2: Ms. Wang is a leader among her peers. Before every test she puts together detailed study sheets and then reviews them with her study group. Although she studies every day by herself, she understands the importance of learning with others and also helping others to learn.

4. How does what you know about the student relate to his or her intended major and/or career path?

How to use #4: If the teacher has information that is relevant it should be included. Refer to example b to see how a recommendation letter can commend a student even if he or she has an undecided major and/or career path. Both of the examples used below work well in recommendation letters.

    a. Mr. Han: Chemistry major, doctor

      i. Mr. Han has told me that he works so hard in my class because he believes that Chemistry is useful to building a foundation in medicine. Since taking my class, he has expressed interest in becoming a Chemistry major and a pre-med student so that he can one day become a doctor. I believe that he is truly interested in both of these fields. He will be a phenomenal chemist in college and a great doctor later.

    b. Ms. Wang: Undecided major, open career path

      i. Ms. Wang is a wonderful student. Regardless of whichever major she hopes to pursue in college, I know she will work hard and do well.

5. Is there any additional information that we should know about this student?

How to use #5: Refer to example a to see how an extra-curricular activity is linked to his major and future career path.

    a. Mr. Han: Volunteers at a near by clinic

        i. Paragraph: Since Mr. Han knows that my wife is a doctor he has asked me for advice on volunteering. I put him in touch with my wife's clinic and he has been volunteering at United Family Hospital in Shanghai for five months now. My wife tells me that he has been extremely helpful. Mr. Han himself has told me that he has been particularly interested in assisting elderly patients. I know that this volunteer work has given him substantial knowledge of what exactly a doctor's work includes and has helped him come to an educated decision about his future profession.

    b. Ms. Wang: Nothing to add (This section will be left out.)

6. How would you sum up this student in one sentence?

    a. Mr. Han: Mr. Han is a dedicated young man who will definitely make an excellent student at your university.

    b. Ms. Wang: Ms. Wang is a bright, young woman with unlimited potential, and will benefit from and contribute to your university.

7. If you speak English and are willing to have an admissions officer speak to you on behalf of the student, please write yes here.

Most recommendation letters from students in the United States state: "Should you require any additional information, please contact me." Recommendation letters provided by Asian international students do not have to necessarily include this line if their teachers do not speak English. Admissions officers understand how rare it is and will not penalize students if their teachers do not include this line. Look at the following examples for an instance when a teacher (a) cannot speak English and (b) can.

    a. Mr. Han: (Left blank. This section will be left out.)

    b. Ms. Wang: Yes

        i. Sentence: Should you require any additional information, please contact me.

Acing the App

8. What is your full name, title, work address, work email address, and work phone number?

    a. Mr. Han: Han Zhi, Chemistry Teacher, ADDRESS, hz@123.com, +86 145-203-234X

    b. Ms. Wang: Jia Tang, Literature Teacher & Assistant Counselor, ADDRESS, jt1352@123.com, +86 145-203-234X

Inputting the Fill-In Question Form

The answers to the above questions can be inputted to make a recommendation letter.

The Basic Format

Recommendation Letter Example 1:

To Whom It May Concern:

I highly recommend NAME OF STUDENT to NAME OF UNIVERSITY. 1. 2. Because of these characteristics, I know he/she will make a wonderful contribution to NAME OF UNIVERSITY.

3. (Example 1)

4. (Example 2)

5. (Not necessary)

To sum up, 6. I wholeheartedly recommend him/her to your school. 7. (Not necessary)

Sincerely,

Signature

8.

Recommendation Letter Example 2:

Dear Admissions Officers:

I am a teacher at HIGH SCHOOL NAME. 1. 2. I know NAME OF STUDENT will make a wonderful contribution to your school.

3. (Example 1)

4. (Example 2)

5. (Not necessary)

Because 6., I recommend him/her to you without reservation. 7.

Regards,

Signature

8.

Samples of Recommendation Letters

I have inputted Mr. Han's fill-in question information into Recommendation Letter Example 1 and Ms. Wang's fill-in question information into Recommendation Letter Example 2. These are good examples that can help inform students, parents and teachers about what an American college admissions recommendation letter looks like.

Recommendation Letter for Mr. Han

To Whom It May Concern:

I highly recommend Mr. Bin Han to the University of Notre Dame. I have known Mr. Han for two years. I first met him when he enrolled in my Chemistry class. Mr. Han is an extremely hardworking student, a self-motivator and a pleasure to have in class. Because of these characteristics, I know he will make a wonderful contribution to the University of Notre Dame.

Mr. Han is an exemplary student who not only thinks of himself but also of his fellow classmates. SInce Mr. Han has extraordinary skills of memorization, he received a flawless score on our periodic table exam. On the other hand, he noticed that two of his peers had not found it as easy. Since their scores were so low, he petitioned me to give them extra credit points to count towards their score if they could get full marks on a makeup test. I allowed it and watched Mr. Han spend every lunch break and two hours after school each day for a week practicing with them. In the end, both students received perfect scores. Mr. Han has assisted his classmates in a similar fashion on two other occasions.

Not only does Mr. Han know how to lead his classmates and give them a helping hand, Mr. Han also knows how to ask for help when he needs it. One day after a second lesson on oxidation and reduction reactions, Mr. Han approached me after school to tell me that he had been having trouble understanding the equations. He came back every day during lunch until the test date and worked on additional problems with me. By the time the test came around, he did well. I believe that this experience is an example of Mr. Han being proactive. He did not wait until he had a bad test score, but rather immediately recognized that he was having trouble and sought help.

Mr. Han has told me that he works so hard in my class because he believes that Chemistry is useful in building a foundation in medicine. Since taking my class, he has expressed interest in becoming a Chemistry major and a pre-med student so that he can one day become a doctor. I believe that he is truly interested in both these fields. He will be a phenomenal chemist in college and a great doctor later.

Since Mr. Han knows that my wife is a doctor he has asked me for advice on volunteering. I put him in touch with my wife's clinic and he has been volunteering at United Family Hospital in Shanghai for five months now. My wife tells me that he has been extremely helpful. Mr. Han himself has told me that he has been particularly interested in assisting elderly patients. I know that this volunteer work has given him substantial knowledge of what exactly a doctor's work includes and has helped him come to an educated decision about his future profession.

To sum up, Mr. Han is a dedicated young man who will definitely make an excellent student at your university. I wholeheartedly recommend him to your school.

Sincerely,

Han Zhi
Chemistry Teacher
ADDRESS
hz@123.com
+86 145-203-234X

Recommendation Letter for Ms. Wang

Dear Admissions Officers:

I am a teacher at Shenzhen High School. I have known Ms. Apple Wang since 2008 when she first took my Traditional Chinese Literature course. Ms. Wang is an exceptionally bright student. She has a unique curiosity of the world that is apparent in the multitude of questions she asks during class. I believe this curiosity helps fuel her dedication to learning. Because she wants to learn as much as possible, she works very hard to memorize all the information and then analyze it to be able to better contribute to class discussions. I know Ms. Wang will make a wonderful contribution to your school.

In China, almost all high schools teach *Dream of the Red Chamber*, a classic Chinese novel. Every year, students write me wonderful papers on themes of a male-dominated society and feudalism in China. Ms. Wang's ten-page essay on the role of women during the Qing dynasty via this novel impressed me and is among one of the best papers I have ever read. Her interpretation of the 12 beauties of Jinling surprised me. I made copies of the essay with comments and without her name. I then passed it out to the class. In this way, my students were able to see a peer example of a good paper and be exposed to the ideas of Ms. Wang.

Ms. Wang is a leader among her peers. Before every test she puts together detailed study sheets and then reviews them with her study group. Although she studies every day by herself, she understands the importance of learning with others and also helping others to learn.

Ms. Wang is a wonderful student. Regardless of whichever major she hopes to pursue in college, I know she will work hard and do well.

Because Ms. Wang is a bright, young woman with unlimited potential and will benefit from and contribute to your university, I recommend her to you without reservation. Should you require any additional information, please contact me.

Regards,

Jia Tang

Literature Teacher & Assistant Counselor

ADDRESS

jt1352@123.com

+86 145-203-234X

Acing the App

The form below is for your teachers to fill out. Schools that ask for recommendation letters typically request for three, one from a counselor and two from teachers. You can copy this form, translate it if necessary, and give it to your teachers to make things easier.

Form

Teacher's Name: _____

Subject: _____

Student's Name: _____

1. How long have you known the student and in what capacity?

_____

_____

_____

_____

_____

_____

_____

2. What adjectives would you use to describe the student?

_____

_____

_____

_____

_____

_____

_____

3. Give two examples from your experience with the student that shows he or she is a good student and would contribute as a student to X University.

_____

_____

_____

_____

_____

_____

4. How does what you know about the student relate to his or her intended major and/or career path?

_____

_____

_____

_____

_____

_____

5. Is there any additional information that we should know about this student?

_____

_____

_____

_____

_____

_____

6. How would you sum up this student in one sentence?

_____

_____

_____

_____

_____

_____

Acing the App

7. If you speak English and are willing to have an admissions officer speak to you on behalf of the student, please write yes here.

_____

8. What is your full name, title, work address, work email address, and work phone number?

_____

_____

_____

_____

_____

_____

12. Acing the Interviews

Not every school offers interviews, but the majority of the most selective colleges prefer to interview their international applicants. Performing well in an interview is a great way to stand out among your peers. Interviews in any language, especially English, are difficult. Thus, it is important to be well prepared. If an alumnus is interviewing you, the interview will generally consist of two parts. The first part focuses on asking the interviewee about their general interests and interest in the college. The second part focuses on asking the interviewer about their time at college. The first part should generally be much longer than the second. In total, interviews should last from 45 minutes to 1 hour and 30 minutes. Because interviews are so difficult, this chapter was written to teach you tricks and tips for performing well at your interviews.

The "actions" part of an interview is the easiest part to prepare for. Nevertheless, my students still have many questions about how they should act. These six tips below should give you the confidence to perform well at your interviews.

Actions

- *Always be punctual.* If the interviewer emails, calls or texts you, make sure to respond within 24 hours. When you have your actual interview, arrive at the location at least five minutes early. These are good common practices that your interviewer may even note in their write-up about you.

- *Dress appropriately.* As a student, you do not have to wear a suit to your interviews unless you want to wear one. However, you should still dress appropriately for your age.

- *Firm handshake and eye contact.* When meeting the interviewer, if you are sitting you should stand, give them a firm handshake, look them in the eyes, introduce yourself, tell them thank you for making the time to meet with you, and then sit back down as they begin to sit. Often times, this direct approach is difficult for students. However, eye contact is especially important in Western culture. Small civilities such as standing when they enter and thanking them for their time are also important. These small actions can help a student begin on a positive note that lasts throughout the rest of the interview.

- *Smile.* A multitude of psychological studies have confirmed the positive effects of smiling. Accordingly, I also encourage my students to smile frequently during interviews. I believe that it makes an interviewee seem friendlier in addition to putting them at ease. A smile also makes an interviewee look like they are enjoying the conversation. It is especially important to smile and show interest when the interviewer is responding to your questions.

- *Be well versed.* The most important part of the interview is what you say to the interviewer. One-word answers and long pauses will not reflect well on you. Thus, it is important to prepare answers to possible questions in advance. In addition, practicing your answers will give you more confidence when speaking English. The ability to speak well in English and to appropriately answer questions are the most important parts of the interview. If you do not feel confident about your English, practicing answers will give you a surge of confidence that will reflect well during your interview regardless of your English speaking capabilities.

- *Follow up.* I always recommend that my students follow up with their interviewer a few hours afterwards through email by sending a brief note. This note should not ask the interviewer how they felt the interview went. It should also not beg

Acing the App

the interviewer to write a good report. A simple thank you email is all that is needed. An example follows:

Dear INTERVIEWER'S NAME,

Thank you for taking the time to meet with me today. I enjoyed talking to you, especially learning about your favorite parts of NAME OF COLLEGE. It has given me a more inclusive perspective of NAME OF COLLEGE. Again, thank you.

Have a wonderful week,

NAME OF STUDENT

Words

The "words" part of the interview is often the most difficult. While students may be able to discuss in detail why a certain major is perfect for them in their native language, students sometimes have trouble with the same terminology in English. Accordingly, it is important to understand what the most likely interview questions are and then practice writing out answers in English. If you need to look up terms, it is important to do so before an interview. Preparing the following questions will help you excel during your interviews. At the end of the chapter, there is a space where you can write your answers. Once you write your answers you should practice saying them out loud as many times as possible. Do not memorize them word for word. This often looks odd during an interview. Become familiar and comfortable with your words instead.

This "words" section is broken up into two parts. The first part includes questions you should be prepared to answer. The second part includes questions you should ask your interviewer. You do not have to spend too much time on the latter. Nevertheless, it is good to not only show that you are capable of having an intelligent conversation, but also that you can be interested in what the other person has to say.

Questions you should be able to sufficiently respond to:

1. What classes are you taking in school right now? Which are your favorites and why?

2. Are you reading any books right now? What is your favorite book? Why?

3. What do you like about your high school? How do you think it has prepared you for college?

4. What motivates you?

5. What would you like to major in? What previous experiences, classes and activities make you interested in this major? Why do you think NAME OF UNIVERSITY has the resources to help you succeed in your major?

6. Why are you interested in NAME OF UNIVERSITY?

7. What are your future goals?

8. What do you think is the most important thing NAME OF UNIVERSITY should know about you?

9. What are your strengths?

10. What difficulties do you feel you have overcome, if any?

Questions to ask the interviewer if he or she is an alumnus:

1. What was your favorite part of college?

2. How is the atmosphere at NAME OF UNIVERSITY?

3. Do you feel the teachers are helpful there?

4. What can you tell me about NAME OF THE CITY THE UNIVERSITY IS IN?

5. Do students frequently collaborate? OR Do you feel students support one another?

Questions to ask the interviewer if he or she works at the admissions office or is a faculty member:

1. In what ways are the teachers helpful at NAME OF UNIVERSITY?

2. What can you tell me about NAME OF THE CITY THE UNIVERSITY IS IN?

3. Do students frequently collaborate? OR Do you feel students support one another?

Acing the App

Fill-In Section

Make sure to include as many specific details as possible. If there are words you do not know how to express, look them up, write them here and circle them so that you know to memorize them for the interview.

1. What classes are you taking in school right now? Which are your favorites and why?

_____

_____

_____

_____

_____

_____

_____

_____

_____

_____

2. Are you reading any books right now? What is your favorite book? Why?

_____

_____

_____

_____

_____

_____

_____

_____

_____

_____

3. What do you like about your high school? How do you think it has prepared you for college?

_____

_____

_____

_____

_____

_____

_____

_____

_____

_____

4. What motivates you?

_____

_____

_____

_____

_____

_____

_____

_____

_____

5. What would you like to major in? What previous experiences, classes and activities made you interested in this major? Why do you think NAME OF UNIVERSITY has the resources to help you succeed in your major?

_____

_____

_____

_____

_____

_____

_____

_____

_____

6. Why are you interested in NAME OF UNIVERSITY?

_____

_____

_____

_____

_____

_____

_____

_____

_____

7. What are your future goals?

_____

_____

_____

_____

_____

_____

_____

_____

_____

_____

8. What do you think is the most important thing NAME OF UNIVERSITY should know about you?

_____

_____

_____

_____

_____

_____

_____

_____

_____

9. What are your strengths?

_____

_____

_____

_____

_____

_____

_____

_____

_____

10. What difficulties do you feel you have overcome, if any?

_____

_____

_____

_____

_____

_____

_____

_____

_____

Appendix: Reading List

By no means is this a complete list. Rather, it is a compilation of various reading lists sent to me by Ivy League friends when posed the question: "What are the quintessential canon of classics?" Nevertheless, please use the following suggestions to begin to prepare yourself or your child for college application success.

Ages 3–7

- *Alexander and the Terrible, Horrible, No Good, Very Bad Day* by Judith Viorst and Ray Cruz

- *Amazing Grace* by Mary Hoffman and Caroline Binch

- Books by Dr. Seuss

- *Brown Bear, Brown Bear, What Do You See?* by Bill Martin, Jr. and Eric Carle

- *Chicka Chicka Boom Boom* by Bill Martin, Jr., John Archambault and Lois Ehlert

- *Corduroy* by Don Freeman

- Curious George books by H.A. Rey

- *Everyone Poops* by Taro Gomi and Amanda Mayer

- *Goodnight Moon* by Margaret Wise Brown

- *If You Give a Mouse a Cookie* by Laura Joffe Numeroff and Felicia Bond

- *Love You Forever* by Robert Munsch and Sheila McGraw

- *Madeline* by Ludwig Bemelmans

- *Miss Nelson is Missing!* by Harry Allard and James Marshall

- *On the Night You Were Born* by Nancy Tillman

- *Once Upon a Potty* by Alona Frankel

- *Pat the Bunny* by Dorothy Kunhardt

- *Stellaluna* by Janell Cannon

- *The Giving Tree* by Shel Silverstein

- *The Little Engine That Could* by Watty Piper and Loren Long

- *The Rainbow Fish* by Marcus Pfister

- *The Tale of Peter Rabbit* by Beatrix Potter

- *The Very Hungry Caterpillar* by Eric Carle

- *Where the Wild Things Are* by Maurice Sendak

- *Zen Shorts* by Jon J. Muth

Ages 8–13

- Books by C.S. Lewis

- Books by Judy Blume

- Books by Mercer Mayer

- Books by Roald Dahl

- Captain Underpants series by Dav Pilkey

- *Charlotte's Web* by E.B. White

- Hardy Boys mysteries by Franklin W. Dixon

Acing the App

- Harry Potter series by J.K. Rowling

- *Hatchet* by Gary Paulsen

- Nancy Drew series by Carolyn Keene

- *Number the Stars* by Lois Lowry

- Percy Jackson and the Olympians series by Rick Riordan

- *Robinson Crusoe* by Daniel Defoe

- *The Adventures of Tom Sawyer* by Mark Twain

- *The Diary of a Young Girl* by Anne Frank

- *The Hobbit* by J.R.R. Tolkein

- *The House on Mango Street* by Sandra Cisneros

- *The Jungle Book* by Rudyard Kipling

Ages 14–Graduation (Includes books, blogs, and magazines)

- *Chinese Undergraduates in the United States* (www.cuus.org)

- *College Confidential* (www.CollegeConfidential.com)

- *Forbes* (www.forbes.com)

- *Gawker* (www.gawker.com)

- *TechCrunch* (www.techcrunch.com)

- *The Economist* (www.economist.com)

- *The New York Times* (www.newyorktimes.com)

- *The Wall Street Journal* (www.wsj.com)

- *Wikipedia* (www.wikipedia.com)

- *100 Years of Solitude* by Gabriel Garcia Marquez

- *1984* by George Orwell

- *A Tale of Two Cities* by Charles Dickens

- *Adventures of Huckleberry Finn* by Mark Twain

- *Aesop's Fables* by Aesop

- *Angels and Demons* by Dan Brown

- *Animal Farm* by George Orwell

- *Anthem* by Ayn Rand

- Anything and everything by Shakespeare

- *Atlas Shrugged* by Ayn Rand

- *Brave New World* by Aldous Huxley

- *Breakfast of Champions* by Kurt Vonnegut

- *Candide* by Voltaire

- *Cat's Cradle* by Kurt Vonnegut

- *Catch-22* by Joseph Heller

- *Confessions* by Saint Augustine

- *Crime and Punishment* by Fyodor Dostoyevsky

- *Cyrano de Bergerac* by Edmond Rostand

- *Fahrenheit 451* by Ray Bradbury

- *Frankenstein* by Mary Shelley

- *Great Expectations* by Charles Dickens

- *Heart of Darkness* by Joseph Conrad

- *Jane Eyre* by Charlotte Bronte

- *Les Miserables* by Victor Hugo

- *Lolita* by Vladimir Nabokov

Acing the App

- *Lord of the Flies* by William Golding

- *Metamorphoses* by Ovid

- *Notes from the Underground* by Fyodor Dostoyevsky

- *Of Mice and Men* by John Steinbeck

- *Pride and Prejudice* by Jane Austen

- *Sense and Sensibility* by Jane Austen

- Short stories by Isaac Asimov

- Short stories by Ray Bradbury

- *Slaughterhouse-Five* by Kurt Vonnegut

- *The Aeneid* by Virgil

- *The Awakening* by Kate Chopin

- *The Bell Jar* by Sylvia Plath

- *The Bluest Eyes* by Toni Morrison

- *The Bonfire of the Vanities* by Tom Wolfe

- *The Catcher in the Rye* by J.D. Salinger

- *The Count of Monte Cristo* by Alexandre Dumas

- *The Da Vinci Code* by Dan Brown

- *The Fountainhead* by Ayn Rand

- *The Great Gatsby* by F. Scott Fitzgerald

- *The Handmaid's Tale* by Margaret Atwood

- *The Iliad* by Homer

- *The Inferno* by Dante Alighieri

- *The Jungle* by Upton Sinclair

- *The Loved One* by Evelyn Waugh

- *The Metamorphosis* by Franz Kafka

- *The Odyssey* by Homer

- *The Old Man and the Sea* by Ernest Hemingway

- *The Scarlet Letter* by Nathaniel Hawthorne

- *The Stranger* by Albert Camus

- *The Trial* by Franz Kafka

- *The Wasteland* by T.S. Eliot

- *Things Fall Apart* by Chinua Achebe

- *This Side of Paradise* by F. Scott Fitzgerald

- *To the Lighthouse* by Virginia Woolf

- *Ulysses* by James Joyce

- *Zen and the Art of Motorcycle Maintenance: An Inquiry into Values* by Robert M. Pirsig